ULISSE ALDROVANDI

Books in the RENAISSANCE LIVES series explore and illustrate the life histories and achievements of significant artists, rulers, intellectuals and scientists in the early modern world. They delve into literature, philosophy, the history of art, science and natural history and cover narratives of exploration, statecraft and technology.

Series Editor: François Quiviger

ULISSE ALDROVANDI
Naturalist and Collector

PETER MASON

REAKTION BOOKS

To Lucia Tongiorgi Tomasi and Giuseppe Olmi

Published by Reaktion Books Ltd
Unit 32, Waterside
44–48 Wharf Road
London N1 7UX, UK
www.reaktionbooks.co.uk

First published 2023

Printed and bound in India by Replika Press Pvt. Ltd

A catalogue record for this book is available from the British Library

ISBN 978 1 78914 717 9

COVER: Anonymous, *Ulisse Aldrovandi*, 17th century, oil on canvas. Museo di Palazzo Poggi, Università di Bologna, photo © Marco Ravenna/Bridgeman Images.

CONTENTS

ABBREVIATIONS

ANT Delle statue antiche, che per tutta Roma, in diversi luoghi, e case si veggono, in Lucio Mauro, Le antichità della città di Roma . . . (Venice, 1556), pp. 115–316

BUB Biblioteca Universitaria Bologna

DP De piscibus libri V et De cetis lib. unus, ed. Johannes Cornelis Uterwer (Bologna, 1638)

MH Monstrorum historia cum Paralipomena accuratissima historiae omnium animalium, ed. Bartolomeo Ambrosini (Bologna, 1642)

MM Musaeum metallicum in libros IIII distributum, ed. Bartolomeo Ambrosini (Bologna, 1648)

ORN Ornithologiae hoc est de avibus historiae libri XII, Ornithologiae tomus alter, and Ornithologiae tomus tertius, ac postremus (Bologna, 1599, 1600 and 1603)

QBH Quadrupedum omnium bisulcorum historia (Bologna, 1621)

Preface

Few public thoroughfares and piazze in Italy are named after the Renaissance natural scientist Ulisse Aldrovandi (1522–1605), who planned to publish a vast encyclopaedia of the natural world, so vast that he was unable to complete most of it during his own lifetime. The Via Ulisse Aldrovandi in the city of Rome gestures towards this scientific activity in its proximity to the Museo Civico di Zoologia and the Bioparc. Aldrovandi's scientific project depended on what was primarily a personal study collection, and it is in Aldrovandi's home town of Bologna that we find the Piazza Ulisse Aldrovandi, located near the university and Palazzo Poggi, the urban mansion that has been the repository since 1742 of a large part of Aldrovandi's collection. That immense collection of *naturalia* and their images has featured prominently in all the major histories of collecting. In 1908 Julius von Schlosser mentioned Aldrovandi in the context of scientific collections in Italy, although the distinction he drew between the princely Kunst- und Wunderkammern of northern Europe and the scientific collections of the south is no longer tenable. Almost eighty years later two of the chapters in the seminal volume *The Origins of Museums*, which may be said to have triggered the surge of interest in the history of collections over the past three decades, highlighted Aldrovandi's importance as a collector.[1]

It is very appropriate for his name to appear in a series called Renaissance Lives, because although the focus of this book is

1 Bartolomeo Passerotti (attrib.), *Ulisse Aldrovandi*, 1582–5, oil on canvas.

on Ulisse Aldrovandi and his collection, he was at the centre of a network involving many other lives. First there was what we might call the Aldrovandi workshop in Bologna. Assisted by his second wife, Francesca Fontana, and a number of amanuenses and artists who worked for him for many years, he was at the centre of a collective enterprise aimed above all at accumulation: the accumulation of knowledge and of objects that came to form the largest collection of *naturalia* in sixteenth-century Europe.

But far wider was the national and even international network involved in collaboration with him. Some of his direct correspondents – the itinerant Charles de l'Écluse (Carolus Clusius), Joachim Camerarius in Germany, Nicolas-Claude Fabri de Peiresc in France – lived far away, but Aldrovandi also knew how to draw on contacts from every walk of life within the Italian peninsula. Lying largely outside the scientific institutions of the day, but with a vast reservoir of local information based on hands-on examination and testing, they gave Aldrovandi access to a wide-ranging network from which he, like a spider at the centre of a web, could spin his voluminous works.[2]

The present work relies heavily on the correspondence between Aldrovandi and these individuals scattered all over the country, from Florence with the grand residences and collections of the Grand Dukes of Tuscany to 'out of the way Pistoia, where there is nothing noteworthy to be seen', as one of his correspondents lamented.[3] I hope the reader will not get lost amid the plethora of unfamiliar names, but their very presence is a reminder of the importance of individuals from all walks of life for the formation of Aldrovandi's collection. A relatively small city like Mantua, bounded on three sides by water, was the home of the pharmacist Filippo Costa, the physicians Giovanni Battista Cavallara and Paolo Carazzi, the surgeon and collector of medicinal plants Ippolito Geniforti della Sirena, the painter at the

Gonzaga court Teodoro Ghisi, and the lawyer with a botanical garden Francesco Borsati. None of them would be expected to appear in a portrait gallery of famous scholars and scientists alongside such icons as Galileo Galilei,[4] but many of these men were collectors, and they all corresponded with Aldrovandi.[5] The same is true of Ferrara, where the Este court showed an interest in the New World from the first and where a number of Aldrovandi's correspondents lived.[6] The much larger city of Bologna was no different in this respect.[7]

Reliance on the letters offers a number of advantages. It is above all a *direct* contact, and one that spans more than fifty years of Aldrovandi's life. In volume it is surpassed by the published works, but as we shall see, most of these were published posthumously, in one case more than sixty years after his death, and they incorporate numerous additions by his editors that do not necessarily reflect his own views. In other words, though valuable in themselves, apart from the youthful work on ancient statues in Rome and the volumes on ornithology, they are too static and far removed from Aldrovandi himself to be able to offer us the dynamism and personal glimpses of his opinions and character that the letters contain.

The letters are, perhaps predictably, sparse on details of his family life. His father, Teseo, died in 1529, leaving his widow to care for six children: Ulisse, Floriano, Achille, Cornelia, Isabella and Lucrezia. When Achille took holy orders, he changed his name to Teseo in memory of his dead father. The loss of the name Achille to the family was remedied when Ulisse named his illegitimate son Achille in 1560. Three years later Ulisse married Paola Macchiavelli, who died in the spring of 1565, but within six months he had remarried, this time to Francesca Fontana. The two children born of this second marriage died in childhood, and in 1577 his son Achille died too, leaving Aldrovandi without any direct descendants. But it was above all a self-image that he was fashioning through his correspondence, his museum and villa, and his publications.

Between 1550 and 1551, the young painter Pellegrino Tibaldi decorated the ceilings of two rooms on the ground floor of Palazzo Poggi with scenes from the Homeric return voyage of Ulysses, an increasingly popular subject in the course of the century. It is very likely that Ulisse Aldrovandi would have been familiar and identified with these images of the exploits of his namesake in an era when names were believed to influence destinies. He may also have identified with the figure of Ulysses in Dante's *Inferno*, who felt impelled to embark on his final and fatal voyage to a 'new land' (*nova terra*), for, as we shall see, Aldrovandi vainly hoped to lead a scientific expedition to explore the wonders of the New World.[8]

THERE IS NO MONOGRAPHIC publication on Ulisse Aldrovandi in any language. Paula Findlen's *Possessing Nature: Museums, Collecting, and Scientific Culture in Early Modern Italy*, published in 1994, is one of the few books in English to deal with Aldrovandi at any length, although, as the subtitle indicates, the scope of her book is much wider. But most of the scholarly literature on Aldrovandi has been written by Italians, and most of it is in Italian. Fundamental for the relation between art and science in Aldrovandi's work are the writings of Giuseppe Olmi and Lucia Tongiorgi Tomasi, while Alessandro Tosi and many others have made valuable contributions too.

It is with a deep debt of gratitude that I have made use of their writings in preparing the present work. It was written during the restrictions necessitated by the outbreak of the COVID-19 pandemic, when access to libraries or archives was impossible. I have therefore had to rely on the literature directly accessible to me in print, including those parts of the correspondence that have been published, assisted by the generous provision of digital files whenever requested to fill in some of the gaps.

Given the target audience of this work, I have translated all original texts into English and referred to the scanty English-language publications where possible. Notes have been kept to a minimum. Where recent literature provides copious bibliography extending back in time, I have limited myself to citing that recent literature alone. Dedicated readers will be able to find their way about in the older literature for themselves.

This is not the multi-volume publication that a fully documented scholarly biography would require. But I hope it will encourage those who encounter Ulisse Aldrovandi and the world in which he lived and operated for the first time to delve further.

Housing and Displaying a Collection

here were no princely cabinets of precious objects and curiosities – Kunst- und Wunderkammern – in sixteenth-century Bologna, but the city could boast some collections of curiosities. The jurist Antonio Giganti (1535–1598) had begun to form a collection of *naturalia* during his five years in Ragusa (modern Dubrovnik) as secretary to the Bolognese prelate and humanist Ludovico Beccadelli. After the death of Beccadelli, he entered the service of Cardinal Gabriele Paleotti in Bologna, where he continued to amass a collection of curiosities of the natural world as well as exotic items from America, perhaps stimulated by his friendship with both Aldrovandi and Paleotti as well as the lesser economic demands of such items compared with paintings and antiquities. Their arrangement according to principles of alternation and symmetry suggests a display that was designed more to impress visitors than to serve a scientific purpose.[1]

Giganti's collection was housed in a palazzo overlooking the Piazza Santo Stefano, not far from the home of the other main collector in sixteenth-century Bologna, Ulisse Aldrovandi. His house and garden were located in the area of Bologna then known as the Borgo Vivaro, which owed its name to its use in former times as a supply basin of fish for the Benedictine monks of the nearby abbey of Santo Stefano. During the Middle Ages the area was built up and became a residential centre of the noble

2 Museum of Francesco Calzolari in Verona, from Benedetto Ceruti, *Musaeum Franc. Calceolarii iun. Veronensis* (1622).

Bolognese families, notably the Pepoli, hence its present name
Via de' Pepoli. This is where what was probably the largest scientific collection of sixteenth-century Europe was housed and
displayed. In 1567 Aldrovandi already had 4,300 dried plants
preserved in thirteen volumes and more than 5,000 other items;[2]
the collection was later reputed to contain no fewer than 18,000
separate items. Reconstructions of the collection, based on
Aldrovandi's successive catalogues of what was a changing display as new objects arrived, give an idea of how it was arranged
in the various rooms on the first floor of the building. However,
one of the most eloquent accounts of the collection is that provided by Jacopo Antonio Buoni, a physician from Ferrara, in a
work published a year after the earthquake that shook that city
in 1570:

> I firmly believe that both now and in the future he has
> few equals in the world in a similar profession. With his
> noble talent, at a personal expense of already more than
> six thousand ducats, and with the help of many secular
> princes and prelates of the church, of learned men of
> various countries, and from his many journeys to places
> near and far, like a new Ulysses, he has observed, seen
> and collected innumerable *naturalia*. He has either the
> skeleton or at least the painting, done from life and in
> its natural colours by his student called the Painter of
> Birds, so skilful in depicting *naturalia* that I would almost
> have called it nature itself, whom he seeks to rival with
> his brush and sets such lifelike *naturalia* before your eyes
> that observers are sometimes deceived, not being able to
> distinguish what is artificial from what is natural . . .
> Whoever enters the museum of Aldrovandi can, without
> the need to travel, see in real life or expertly copied in
> painting the riches of the sea and the land, true minerals,

semi-minerals, concretions, jewels, marbles, stones, earth, entire plants and their parts such as exudations, juices, capillaries and resins, fruits, flowers, seeds, roots, barks, precious woods, the aromatics from the Indies and exotic plants from the New World, the teeth and horns of animals from very remote countries, domestic quadrupeds and wild animals, birds, fishes, shells and marine monsters and serpents. In short, his museum is a compendium of the *naturalia* that are found beneath and above the earth, in the air and in water.[3]

A visitor's first impression of Aldrovandi's museum was provided by the skeletal remains of a whale. Guillaume Rondelet had admired the bones of a sperm whale displayed in front of the Palazzo della Signoria in Florence, a widespread practice throughout Europe, and the Bolognese collector would not have wanted to be outdone. Opportunities for obtaining such a trophy were provided every time a whale was found beached on the Italian shores, as happened in Ancona in 1584, and Aldrovandi had a bowl made from whalebone that was a gift from the Bolognese artist Bartolomeo Passarotti or a member of his family (*DP*, p. 685).[4] The whale was accompanied by other marine creatures, including a monstrous fish that Aldrovandi knew was a hoax. At the same time, exhibiting a dried fish that he knew to be an artificial concoction makes Aldrovandi something of a showman, anticipating the dramatic presentation of the museum of natural history of Charles Willson Peale in Philadelphia in the nineteenth century.[5]

After passing through the vestibule of Aldrovandi's display area, a visitor would find two rooms that served to accommodate the numerous unbound coloured drawings used for the preparation of woodblocks, as well as some of the blocks themselves, either already incised or waiting to be incised by the block-cutter.

Aldrovandi's collection of some 3,900 printed books and more than three hundred manuscripts was housed in the two private rooms of the library, with some overflow into the other two rooms. Only a few visitors would have been admitted to these private working areas.

The fifth and largest room, illuminated like the two library rooms by a window, was the museum proper. Here too first impressions were important: one of the commonest American items to be found in the European collections of natural history, the armadillo, was placed above the entrance, while the doorway area included a stork, a sturgeon, an alcion (known from medieval bestiaries, the alcion is sometimes identified as a gull or kingfisher) and a bull ray. These were all spectacular in some way: the alcion was believed to make a floating nest on the sea and to calm the waters around the time of the winter solstice (the 'halcyon days'). The stork, noted for its care for its young and their care for their parents in old age, was not known to nest in Italy, so its presence in Aldrovandi's collection would have made it an unusual visitor. It was often represented with a snake or frog in its beak; as a wader, it was, like the alcion, a bird that bridged the elements of air and water. As for the sturgeon and the bull ray, the former is the largest freshwater fish, while the latter, described by Pierre Belon as the largest of the rays, can reach a length of 1.5 metres (5 ft).

A visitor who stood in the uncluttered centre of the room would have been able to survey the collection of plants, animals and minerals grouped by category that lined the walls or were suspended from the nine beams of the ceiling. Besides a large number of fishes, the beams accommodated some of the most unfamiliar items of the collection. These items, which were presumably added in the order in which they arrived, formed a heterogeneous ensemble that included not only marine creatures such as a skeletal dolphin and a turtle, but plants (sea coconut,

papyrus, white Tuscan wheat) and shells. The crocodile or caiman was a favourite in displays, not only in natural history collections but in churches (illus. 3). Antonio Mascagni wrote to Aldrovandi in 1584 to recount the story of a serpent or basilisk that had been captured in 1503 and suspended from the ceiling of a church in Pisa,[6] and the Bolognese collector had one hanging from a beam, together with the equally popular boxfish. Some of the zoological specimens were actually pharmaceutical items too, such as the hoof of an elk, a gift from Marino Cavalli, who had served as the Venetian ambassador to the Ottoman court in Constantinople. The 'nail of the Great Beast', as it was called, was believed to possess medical properties as an anti-epileptic, and its exotic provenance gave it added allure.

Smaller items, including minerals and coins, were arranged on shelves around the walls: a statuette of Venus with Cupid and a dolphin by Giambologna, court sculptor to the Medici; a Palissy-style figurine by Timoteo Refati of 'a green lizard cast in white lead, which is cast and finished in such a lifelike manner that it

3 Crocodile affixed to the wall of Santuario de la Fuensanta, Córdoba, Spain, since at least 1618.

almost seems to breathe';[7] casts of small sculptures by Alfonso Lombardi and others; decorated shells, scientific instruments, small wooden models, optical illusion mirrors, and Aldrovandi's scanty collection of antiquities.

The two rooms of the library were not entirely free of such items either, since the skeleton of a dog was placed above the entrance to one of them. Their close proximity to the central exhibition area underlined the circularity that Aldrovandi saw between the activities of observing and writing. Though documentation is lacking, small items from the central exhibition area would undoubtedly have found their way into the library from time to time for closer study. Such observation of the individual items would lead to their insertion in his voluminous manuscripts and later publications, while the storehouse of knowledge contained in the books of his library provided the instrument necessary for understanding those objects themselves in light of what earlier authors such as Pliny and Aristotle had written. This information was excerpted and copied on to scraps of paper that Aldrovandi and his assistants then arranged alphabetically to serve as an aide-mémoire for the compilation of his voluminous works.

The familiar, widely reproduced image of the museum of Francesco Calzolari in Verona (illus. 2) conveys something of the nature of Aldrovandi's display: there are the marine animals suspended from the beams of the ceiling, stuffed birds arranged on top of the cupboards that line the walls, and a variety of smaller items of the natural world (including petrified fossil fish from Bolca) and crafted items on the shelves. However, that image comes from the catalogue of the Calzolari collection commissioned by his grandson from two local physicians and published in 1622 with a dedication to the Gonzaga in Mantua, and should not be taken to reflect accurately the contents of the original Calzolari collection that Aldrovandi visited in 1571, even if it probably displayed the same variety.

Closer to Calzolari's own time is the description of his museum by Borgarutio Borgarucci. This translator and editor inserted the description between a translation into Italian of the annotated Latin edition of the work of the Portuguese physician Garcia de Orta by Charles de l'Ecluse, and a translation into Italian of the work of the Spanish physician Nicolás Monardes. The two works dealt with the medicinal properties of items imported from the Americas and the East. In this Venetian edition published in 1589, Borgarrucci lavishly praised the collecting activities of Calzolari and sketched the riches of his museum beyond the more specifically pharmaceutical items:

> There can be no doubt that, as Francesco is naturally inclined to great courtesy and generosity, he will be only too ready to show it to whoever would like to see the other marvels of various simple and composite medicaments and various minerals, semi-minerals, precious stones, very rare animals, birds that have been seen by few, unknown fishes, various types of soil, wood and objects extracted from the earth of every kind – in short, all that can be seen that is beautiful, rare and good among the most learned and keen intellects of our time. They can be found there as if in a universal theatre of all the most exquisite and singular things in the world.[8]

Besides lapis lazuli and other stones with remarkable veining and a variety of bezoars, Borgarucci also mentioned petrifactions, asbestos thread (for which Calzolari had been pestering Camerarius in several letters from the 1580s), three pieces of unicorn horn given to him by Emperor Maximilian, 'a tablet full of hieroglyphic letters, many Egyptian idols, all inscribed with similarly hiero-glyphic letters', a piece of Egyptian papyrus 'written in letters that no one understands', a bird of paradise without feet or wings and another creature that was believed to live on air, the chameleon, all kinds of falcons, shells, 'and other very beautiful things that would be too many to mention them all here'.

In a comparison of Aldrovandi's exhibition space with that of Calzolari, the latter is clearly no mere adjunct to the pharmacy; its exotic rarities were evidence of the breadth of the materials on which he could draw to produce his famous theriac and other compounds. Aldrovandi's collection also served this purpose when he needed to substantiate the claims regarding the Bolognese theriac. However, his status was different from that of Calzolari, and it was primarily as an object to be viewed by distinguished visitors, as well as serving his own scientific interests, that the Bolognese collection was presented. Moreover, the many visits during his lifetime by artists who were not directly connected with Aldrovandi's workshop are evidence that the aesthetic impact of the collection was not absent from his mind either, while the fact that he kept two visitors' books, one for the most distinguished visitors and the other for the rest, is a clear sign of his claim to elevated status. Not that questions of status were absent from Calzolari's mind either: after the 1571 visit, Calzolari wrote to Aldrovandi begging for some rarity for his studio, 'so that I will have occasion to say that I had this rarity from Signor Aldrovandi'.[9] And when he heard that Joachim Camerarius had Conrad Gessner's material on plants in his possession, he could hardly wait to see his name mentioned there.[10]

The static impression that the catalogues and frontispieces convey is deceptive, as these were dynamic collections. Some items may have deteriorated over time and had to be removed, while the constant flow of new items, especially from the New World, made it impossible to maintain rigid spatial distinctions. The same phenomenon can be observed in the collection of coloured drawings that Aldrovandi commissioned or received from others. They display no apparent order, since they were produced each time that a new and noteworthy item arrived. This also goes some way to explaining why most of Aldrovandi's publications appeared posthumously. It was only after the flow of new acquisitions began to decrease, in inverse proportion to the growth of Aldrovandi's collection itself, that it became possible to take stock and to compile an orderly presentation.

Visitors to Bologna today can still see a number of items from Aldrovandi's collection. For example, an African lizard, a guitar shark, the head of a porbeagle shark and the jaw of a monkfish are displayed together with the incised woodblocks used for printing images of them. A sizeable part of the collection, however, was dismantled and dispersed in the nineteenth century, and what remains is divided between various university departments and museums in the city. Some items, such as the Amazonian axe now in a Roman museum, travelled even further – another reminder that the history of collections is by no means static.

HÆC VISVNTVR ROMÆ, IN HORTO CARD. A VALLE, EIVS BENEFICIO, EX ANTIQVITATIS, RELIQVIIS IBIDEM CONSERVAT

ONE

Finding His Way: The Early Years

 hen the eleven-year-old Ulisse Aldrovandi ran away from home in Bologna to Rome in 1534, he had already lived through a decade of profound change. The combined German and Spanish mercenaries of Charles V had plundered and pillaged their way down the Italian peninsula and sacked Rome in 1527. The subsequent crowning of Charles in Bologna in 1530 during a meeting with Pope Clement VII seemed to herald the dawn of a new era of peace and stability. The world was watching – Pietro Bembo referred to the city at the time as the 'world's theatre'. That world had been shaken up by the breakaway Protestant movement within the Church, and there were hopes that the promise to reform the Church and to restore its original form would be made good by this new alliance.

In a letter of 1527, Erasmus had used the term *novus mundus* to refer to the new world envisaged by the Lutheran Reformation. The term had first been applied to the newly discovered continent of America by Amerigo Vespucci at the beginning of the century, and that new world was visibly present in Bologna when foreign delegations bearing exotic gifts arrived in the city for the second meeting between Charles and Clement in 1532–3. One of these was a Spanish Dominican friar bearing gifts, including featherworks, carefully crafted stone knives, masks inlaid with turquoise and 'some nicely painted books, which looked like hieroglyphs'.[1]

4 Hieronymus Kock after Maarten van Heemskerck, in *Speculum romanae magnificentiae*, 1553, engraving.

Albrecht Dürer's enthusiastic reaction to the sight of the objects from Mexico that were on display in Brussels in 1520 has often been quoted:

> Further, I have seen the things brought to the King from the new golden land: a sun, wholly of gold, wide a whole fathom, also a moon, wholly of silver and just as big; also two chambers full of their implements, and two others full of their weapons, armour, shooting engines, marvellous shields, strange garments, bedspreads, and all sorts of wondrous things for many uses, much more beautiful to behold than miracles. These things are all so costly that they have been estimated at a hundred thousand florins; and in all the days of my life I have seen nothing which has gladdened my heart so much as these things. For I have seen therein wonders of art, and have marvelled at the subtle *ingenia* of people in far-off lands. And I know not how to express what I have experienced thereby.[2]

It is easy to imagine that the buzz of excitement, the charged atmosphere, the climate of expectation and the display of unfamiliar rare and precious objects from afar must have produced a strong impact on the imagination of the young Ulisse Aldrovandi in the years preceding his precipitous departure for Rome.

His domestic life had been affected by upheaval too. He was born in Bologna on 11 September 1522 to Veronica Marescalchi, who was related to Ugo Boncompagni, later Pope Gregory XIII, through his mother, Angela Marescalchi. Ulisse's father was Teseo Aldrovandi, a lawyer and secretary of the Bolognese Senate. After the death of his father in 1529, the responsibility for the upbringing of Ulisse and his five siblings fell on Veronica, who hired a private tutor for their education.[3]

But though Ulisse was born into a patrician family (one of his ancestors had been the patron of Michelangelo in Bologna in the 1490s), it was not a rich one. The Milanese Girolamo Benzoni, who was only a couple of years older than Aldrovandi, was the author of what was to become an immensely popular account of fifteen years of travel in the New World, *Historia del mondo nuovo*, first published in 1565. In the preface to that work addressed to Pope Pius IV, he described his motivation to undertake that journey in terms of the declining fortune of his family and the curiosity of a young man eager to see the world and especially the riches of the 'newly discovered kingdoms'.[4] Aldrovandi's departure so soon after the death of his father was probably inspired by similar motives: looking back on it in his *Discorso naturale*, when he was around fifty years old, Aldrovandi wrote that he had been 'spurred on from an early age by the thirst for knowledge'.[5] After a four-month stay in Rome as the page of a bishop, he returned to Bologna, but he was soon on the move again, this time to work as a clerk for a merchant in Brescia. After a year in that position, he set out for Rome again – as before, without informing his relatives – but this time his journey took him much further. After falling in with a Sicilian pilgrim, he set his sights on Santiago de Compostela and travelled as far as the church of Santa Maria in Finisterre, where the Virgin Mary was supposed to have appealed to Santiago to encourage his work of conversion. In a later memoir written in the 1580s, Aldrovandi mentions that the journey afforded him the opportunity to observe not only holy relics, but various reptiles and plants.[6] Whether this is what he actually did or whether he is projecting this interest in the natural world back in time is hard to decide. Later still, in 1595, he wrote to Girolamo Mercuriale that when he was a student, his reading of Theophrastus had triggered a strong desire in him to conduct a natural history of Corsica. That ambition had never been fulfilled, but by then he was in his seventies and was delighted that Giuseppe Casabona was being sent on precisely such a mission.[7]

Back home in 1539, his relatives insisted that he abandon his wanderings and study, but he was still reluctant to settle down. In Bologna, he studied jurisprudence and humanities before moving on to medicine, logic, philosophy and mathematics in Padua. This period came to an abrupt end with another journey to Rome, this time summoned by the Inquisition on a charge of heresy. In the middle of the sixteenth century vigorous discussions of Christian doctrine by Anabaptists and others were taking place in the cities of northern Italy, where the bold ideas advanced in those circles gave at least one observer the impression that he had arrived in a 'new world'.[8] On 1 May 1549 Aldrovandi was one of a group of five men accused of being followers of one of the Anabaptists, Camillo Renato. Their status varied from Aldrovandi's family to that of a schoolmaster and a cobbler. They were obliged to repudiate their ideas in a public ceremony in the Basilica of San Petronio, and Aldrovandi, probably because his status would draw more attention to him in the event of conviction and execution, was one of the three who were dispatched to Rome to await trial. The cobbler and the schoolmaster remained in Bologna to serve their sentences; the cobbler, one Bernardo Brascaglia, was later condemned to death for persisting in his heretical views.[9] We shall never know to what extent Aldrovandi's recantation was genuine or whether he was a Nicodemite: the opening scene in the decoration of his suburban villa outside Bologna was that of the feigned madness of Ulysses, his namesake, on which he commented, 'Knowing how to simulate at a certain moment for an honest purpose that is also useful to oneself is a virtue.'[10]

ROME: THE INQUISITION AND THE ANTIQUITIES

The explosive growth of knowledge about the New World in the sixteenth century was matched by a shift in perceptions of the Old World at roughly the same time. Ancient inscriptions had been sporadically collected and monuments noticed before then, but a more influential chance discovery was made in the 1470s by the artists who stumbled across the cavities in the surface of the Oppian Hill in Rome and descended to the level of the top of the rubble beneath. They were stupefied to see the exuberant decoration of what had been Emperor Nero's grand palace, the Domus Aurea, and the new style discovered there, which came to be known as grotesque, rapidly spread through Europe and even into Spanish America.[11]

Some objects came to light by chance during agricultural or building work, while others surfaced as the result of planned excavations. The scholarly input derived from examination of these newly discovered remains of classical antiquity now came to be an element as important as, if not more important than, a heavy dependence on ancient literary sources. At the same time, members of the wealthy elite who not only had sumptuous urban residences but owned property on the outskirts of the city were able to organize excavations on their own private estates. The discovery there of figural nudes and mythological subjects, in particular, came to reflect a shift in taste on the part of these families in the 1470s and 1480s. From then on until the Sack of Rome in 1527, popes and princely members of the Curia began to lay out pleasure gardens populated by figural sculptures.[12]

In the digging that continued in Rome in the first decades of the sixteenth century, one of the most spectacular discoveries was the unearthing of the ancient sculptural ensemble of Laocoön and his sons near the Basilica of Santa Maria Maggiore on 14 January 1506. It was promptly transported to the Vatican Belvedere courtyard and installed in a niche there, and four years later four artists were invited to make a life-size copy of the statue group in wax for casting in bronze. Access to the Vatican sculptures was restricted by Pius IV in the 1560s, but one of those fortunate enough to see the Laocoön group before then was Ulisse Aldrovandi when he visited the Belvedere in 1550, though his dating of its discovery 'in our time' is clearly approximate. Without any authorial preface, he launched straight into his first published work, *Delle statue antiche, che per tutta Roma, in diversi luoghi, & case si veggono* with a description of the Belvedere gardens. *Delle statue antiche* is a list of the objects owned by some eighty collectors in Rome, as well as some of those on public display in squares or churches. It focuses on those located between the Vatican and the Campo Marzio, such as the famous hanging garden of Cardinal Andrea della Valle (illus. 4), but also includes some locations in the green areas (*vigne*) situated outside the centre. This was a time, particularly in Rome, when members of the clergy needed to find ways to promote their importance in a city in which ostentation and status played such an important part. Assembling large quantities of antiquities, preferably of high quality, served this need to impress visitors to their collections and thus to enhance their prestige.

Aldrovandi's compilation, although not illustrated, is a very important source of information about the collections at this time, especially when taken in conjunction with the sketches of different Roman locations, including the objects on show in outdoor collections, done by the Netherlandish artist Maarten van Heemskerck in Rome between 1532 and 1536. For example, the combination of the statue of a silen emptying a wineskin with a large *krater* decorated with erotic scenes, the famous Tazza Torlonia,[13] in the garden created by Paolo Emilio Cesi in the Vatican Borgo is attested by van Heemskerck in 1537 and Aldrovandi thirteen years later. It has even proven possible to reconstruct the layout of the Cesi garden on the basis of the precise details regarding the axial alignment of the statues provided by Aldrovandi and the clear depiction of the same layout in a painting of the garden by Hendrik van Cleve III from 1584, though the visit on which that painting is based must have taken place at around the same time as that of Aldrovandi.[14]

It might be tempting to assume that Aldrovandi had studied antiquities before becoming more engrossed in studies of the natural world, but it would be unjustified to suppose that his interests coincided with those of the present-day scholars who make use of his work to reconstruct the Roman collections of his day. He generally recorded only the most eye-catching items, passing over inscriptions, coins and other pieces that he considered minor works. In fact, his knowledge of antiquities appears to have been rather limited. Most of the descriptions are bare lists of the marbles on display, often with the most rudimentary explanation of mythological or historical figures when identifiable, such as 'Pluto, God of the Underworld'. The utility of such a work is anything but obvious, for those who gained admittance to these mainly aristocratic gardens would have been equally well (if not better) informed about the iconography of the statues. Moreover, Aldrovandi's publication is not illustrated. The middle of the sixteenth century was the moment when 'Italy saw a renewal of the authentic mythographical tradition' in several works published with woodcut images.[15] Nevertheless, given the lengths to which Aldrovandi had to go in later years to secure funding and patronage for his illustrated work on ornithology, at this stage he will simply have lacked the connections and resources to envisage a publishing endeavour on this scale.

Inevitably, there are inaccuracies in Aldrovandi's account. For example, the repeated mention of 'marble slabs with relief decoration' inserted in walls appears to ignore the fact that they were taken from the sides of marble sarcophagi. A Leda and the Swan in the Cesi collection had been cleverly concocted by combining a statue of a crouching Venus with one of a child strangling a goose on a single base; Aldrovandi was fooled into thinking that the group had been cut from a single block of marble. He may be forgiven for having identified the sculptural group known as the Farnese Bull, installed in the Palazzo Farnese only four years before his visit, as one of the labours of Hercules, since the myth of Dirke was unfamiliar to many of those who commented on the work. Likewise, the female statue that he identified as Agrippina the Elder was known as Livia when it entered Syon House in the eighteenth century, and was only later given its current identification as the goddess Aphrodite.[16] In a few cases Aldrovandi is eager to show how up to date he is. Thus, a relief sculpture of a 'very beautiful horse which seems to stumble and fall' in the collection of Antonio Paloso – perhaps to be identified with Marcus Curtius flinging himself into the abyss – was found 'a few days ago in Tivoli' (ANT, p. 212). Moreover, the indication of empty spaces waiting to be filled in the Cesi garden is a reminder that many of these collections were caught up in a process of expansion or dissolution. Many of these snippets of local information, such as the provenance of some of the finds, must have been provided by the guides who escorted him around these collections. Most of these guides have remained anonymous, though Aldrovandi does mention that he was shown around the collection of Girolamo Garimberto by the connoisseur himself. Clearly, as an antiquarian Aldrovandi was far from the level of expertise of his near contemporary Fulvio Orsini, the librarian of the Farnese family and a major collector in his own right, who criticized the practice on the part of careless restorers of joining heads to headless shafts, both of which might be genuine in themselves but which did not originally belong together.

Nevertheless, we have to set Aldrovandi's work within the situation – particularly his personal situation – at the time. It should be remembered that he wrote the work in Rome not because he had chosen to go there to study its antiquities, but because he had been summoned there and imprisoned by the Inquisition. As events turned out, because the opening of the prisons after the death of a pope was a long-standing Roman tradition, the death of Pope Paul III on 10 November 1549 led to Aldrovandi's immediate release. However, he was still under orders to remain in Rome by that same institution. A description of the possessions of some of the wealthiest and most high-ranking families in Rome, presented in the form of an itinerary based on first-person observation by an author who had privileged access to these collections, may have been intended to speak for his good character.

While the shortest entry is that for the collection of Salviati in the Borgo – 'Here there is only the statue of a naked Hercules' – no fewer than 26 pages are devoted to the collection in the residence of Cardinal Rodolfo Pio da Carpi in the Campo Marzio and in his suburban villa on the Quirinale, which he had just purchased from Giacomo Cesi in August 1549. So precise is the information provided by Aldrovandi on the latter that, in retracing Aldrovandi's steps, modern researchers have been able to reconstruct the layout of the Carpi villa and grounds.[17]

As for the objects described in the Carpi urban residence, they are all located in the various study rooms, a further indication of the author's intimacy with one of the most prominent families in Rome. The carefully crafted walnut wall cabinets contained precious manuscripts written in Greek, Hebrew and Arabic, vases, busts, inscriptions, timepieces and portrait paintings by Raphael (the unique mention of paintings among the Roman collections), while there were statues stood outside the cabinets too. As if that were not enough, the account closes with the contents of a storeroom

full of antiquities, mostly made of metal, which it would require a separate book to describe in detail. Here there are many figurines of humans and various animals, lanterns, small vases, many made of glass, stamps for coins, helmets, items of defensive armour, knives, daggers, swords, spearheads, shot, javelins, arrowheads and other ballistic weapons, all of very hard-tempered metal. Surgical medical instruments, seals, keys, rings, brooches and various other clasps, all made of metal and antique, and an ancient glass of pure rock-crystal with very delicate incision, also many other different kinds of things that many days would not suffice to see them, let alone describe them. (ANT, p. 183)

Though not absent from the descriptions of the other collections, superlatives abound – 'most rare', 'most extraordinary', 'very beautiful' – in the accounts of the Carpi properties. Indeed, Aldrovandi goes so far as to call the suburban one, modelled as it was on the pastoral life evoked in Virgil's *Georgics*, a 'terrestrial paradise'.

It has been plausibly suggested that the lavish space devoted to and praise of the Carpi collections were motivated by the fact that the cardinal, one of the six cardinal inquisitors of the Roman Inquisition at this time, was considered a moderate who remained on cordial terms with individuals accused of heresy. In highlighting the collections of this and other high-ranking prelates, there may have been more at stake than the urge to promote his own status. Aldrovandi may have hoped that what was on the surface a catalogue of ancient sculptures in the possession of powerful patrons might prompt the intervention of these same patrons on his behalf during the tense six months after his release from prison.

With the election of Giovanni Maria Ciocchi del Monte as the new pope, Julius III, on 7 February 1550, Aldrovandi may have felt a wave of relief, since del Monte had been a papal legate to Bologna and Aldrovandi seems to have been on good terms with another member of the del Monte family. Indeed, when del Monte was examining the charges brought against Aldrovandi by the Inquisition, he had asked for the case to be tried in Bologna because the mother of the accused was a poor widow who lived on charity. With the Inquisition no longer breathing so heavily down his neck and after his return to Bologna in May, Aldrovandi may have felt less of a need to pursue his work on the marble collections in Rome any further. Back in Bologna his liberty was still subject to certain restrictions that were not lifted until March 1553, and his formal absolution was not issued until July 1567, eighteen years after his initial incarceration.[18] He may well have been reluctant to return to Rome during these years; a call for a fresh examination of Aldrovandi by the Congregation of the Inquisition in 1571 does not seem to have had serious repercussions, but must surely have made him uneasy.[19] By 1577, the occasion of his second visit to Rome, the situation had changed yet again: his brother Teseo was *commendatore* of the Ospedale Santo Spirito in Rome, his friend the naturalist Michele Mercati was chief papal physician, and the pope himself was the Bolognese Gregory XIII.

IT WAS NOT UNTIL 1556 that the manuscript was first published, followed by a slightly expanded edition two years later. Many years later, Aldrovandi claimed that he had given it to the Venetian publisher Giordano Ziletti, who had a bookshop in Rome, with the request not to publish it. However, this feigned modesty was probably part of the self-image that he was fashioning in the 1590s, as spurious as the claim that he had gone to Rome to further his studies in philosophy and medicine and had only composed the manuscript for his own entertainment. Though Rodolfo Pio da Carpi was dead by the time of the publication, the book was dedicated to Giulio Martinengo dalla Pallada, who came from the same noble Martinengo family as Carpi's mother. Whether the choice was Ziletti's own or whether

it was a joint decision by author and publisher, it is a significant
one. Aldrovandi was simply doing what anyone else in his position
would have done in that place at that time: appealing for help
to get him out of a difficult situation. The use of the vernacular
is also telling in this respect. While in his later works Aldrovandi
would use Latin, the language of international scholarship and,
hopefully, fame, the Italian language was more appropriate to a
work written for a special, local occasion. One can hardly speak
of a patron–client relationship at this stage, for there is no indication that the protection he sought was in any way intended to
be long lasting or even permanent.

IT EMERGES FROM these considerations that the quest for
continuity between Aldrovandi's interest in antiquities and his
later studies of the natural world is in vain. Certainly, he read
and annotated Vitruvius, but he was more concerned with math-
ematical and hydraulic matters than with antiquities as such. He
may even have intended his notes as a study aid for private students since he is not recorded as having lectured on Vitruvius
during his official classes in the Studio di Bologna.[20] The antiquarian and architect Pirro Ligorio was in Rome at the same time
as Aldrovandi, but there is no evidence that the two men met
during the latter's eight-month stay.

Aldrovandi did not devote much of his later life to pursuing
the study of antiquities, and when he did return to annotate his
own copy of *Delle statue antiche*, his comments in the margin, like
those of Pliny before him or of his Dutch correspondent Everard
Vorstius, are of a natural-historical nature.[21] Thirty years after
the event, in the course of the correspondence that he, Pirro
Ligorio and several others conducted with Cardinal Gabriele
Paleotti, he mentioned that he had seen the grotesques in the
Domus Aurea of Nero with his own eyes, 'having torches and

twine with us to avoid getting lost', but there is no evidence of a specifically antiquarian interest at this point.[22] Seventy years after Pintoricchio and other artists had first entered the subterranean interior of the Domus Aurea, buried beneath the baths of Trajan on the Oppian Hill, there was nothing pioneering or even necessarily scientific about Aldrovandi's visit. Though he did write bookishly on the interpretation of some passages in classical texts such as 'Explanation of two passages in Plautus' or 'On the words Taurobolium and Criobolium', only a few of the vast quantity of Aldrovandi manuscripts now in the University Library of Bologna have any bearing on antiquities as such.[23] Examples are one dealing with the weights and measures of the ancients or another on ancient drinking vessels, and the alphabetical list of the contents of his museum is confined to some glass vases, a Roman ceramic vase, some Roman lamps, including one in the shape of an ox's head, some marble sculptures, and two slabs of basalt inscribed with 'hieroglyphs'. We might add the inclusion of two ancient instruments of torture, an *ungula* and an *equuleus* (illus. 5), and a triclinium among the painted drawings.[24] The latter was a popular object of enquiry among antiquarians and appears in the Paper Museum of Cassiano dal Pozzo in the seventeenth century,[25] but if anything, the presence of these few images among a total of almost 3,000 is a sign of just how marginal this field was to Aldrovandi's main interests.

It looks as though Aldrovandi was aware that a gentlemanly collection ought to include some antiquities, but did not spend much time or money on collecting them. Indeed, the mention of these few objects is primarily in terms of the material of which they are made. Although lamps and other small household utensils became increasingly popular in collections towards the end of the sixteenth century because of the light that they could throw on everyday life, Aldrovandi does not appear to have shared this interest. In a similar way, as we shall see, his American artefacts

Equuleus tormentum antiquorum.

5 Ancient torture instrument (*equuleus*), from Aldrovandi's *Tavole*, housed at the Biblioteca Universitaria Bologna.

are appraised in terms of their material composition (feathers, metal, stone and so on) rather than for their use.

All the same, he may have drawn some lessons of a different kind from the Roman collections for the formation of his own. The contents of the Carpi storeroom are made of metal or rock-crystal, anticipating Aldrovandi's own work on minerals, and the very profusion of the Carpi collection could also have been a spur to seek to present above all a vast *quantity* of objects in the collection that Aldrovandi was to form in Bologna. In a similar vein, the tour of the Garimberto collection, considered one of the finest Roman collections at the time, hosted by its owner Girolamo concludes with a description of the objects made of precious stones, bronze, silver and gold, as well as a series of ancient ceramic vases and vases made of black stone and in other colours, but this is not all. To crown it all, there was an object of wonder: a petrified elephant's jaw complete with teeth, as well as petrified wood, shells and the horn of a stag. The petrified elephant parts and the horn occupied that intermediate category between animal and mineral that was to fascinate Aldrovandi for the rest of his life. Whatever the immediate purpose of the compilation may have been, it is clear that his search for protection in the form of a temporary patron did not exclude a genuine interest in the wonders of nature. In the next chapter, we shall see how the period in Rome stimulated that interest and pointed the way to furthering it through exchanges of letters, objects and images with other like-minded individuals in Italy and, eventually, further afield.

TWO

The Network Expands

Though he is unlikely to have appreciated being summoned to Rome to spend several weeks in prison there, Aldrovandi's compulsory stay in the city coincided with the presence of a host of important foreign visitors. The election of a new pope was imminent, and Vatican-watchers from many countries flocked to Rome to await the result, some even hoping to influence it. Among the five French cardinals dispatched to Rome for the conclave was François de Tournon, the patron of a number of young French intellectuals, including his personal apothecary, the botanist Pierre Belon (1517–1564). Another naturalist who was in Rome at the time was Guillaume Rondelet (1507–1566), professor of medicine at the renowned University of Montpellier where François Rabelais also studied and Belon may have done too. In his autobiography, Aldrovandi stated that it was at this time in Rome that 'I began to take an interest in this *cognitione sensata* of plants and more particularly of dried animals, and of the varieties of fish that I often saw on the fish market' with Rondelet.[1] The phrase *cognitione sensata* refers to direct observation through the senses as opposed to book learning; such claims to eyewitness status became increasingly common among natural scientists in the second half of the sixteenth century.

Obtaining that first-hand information was not confined to visiting the fish market, though it does seem to have been a

privileged source of information for physicians and naturalists
at this time. This is easy enough to understand if one remembers
the proximity of Rome to the sea and the scope of the international market to which it was linked, large enough to provoke
rivalry as well as cooperation between (budding) ichthyologists.
In March 1559 the fish expert Ippolito Salviani complained to
Aldrovandi that, although he had welcomed a student called
Pietro from Bologna as a friend and had often taken him to the
market in Rome to show him the fish there, he did not know how
many fish Pietro had dried for him and, to make matters worse,
Pietro had left after Christmas and was now working for a rival.[2]

Aldrovandi's juxtaposition of fish and plants can also be found
in the field trips that Rondelet began to organize with his students in Montpellier, taking them on herborizing expeditions as
well as to the coast. This may have been an earlier tradition in
Montpellier, though the fact that there is no evidence of Rondelet's
having organized such excursions there before his return from
Italy suggests that he may have been inspired by Italian examples,
such as Luca Ghini.[3] Whether Aldrovandi met other naturalists
in Rome is a matter for conjecture. He claimed to have learnt
a lot about fish from Paolo Giovio, but since Giovio left Rome
in the autumn of 1549 this was presumably knowledge derived
from Giovio's treatise on the fish of Rome (*De Romanis piscibus*),
published in 1524, rather than from personal contact.

Knowledge of the properties of plants and herbs was one
of the branches of Rondelet's discipline; the fresh fish on the
Roman market offered an opportunity for another one: anatomy.
Snakes too came within its purview, especially in view of the
importance of vipers as a vital ingredient in the panacea theriac.
Aldrovandi had been able to observe them in Toulouse on his
return journey from Spain. Moreover, the Dutch physician and
naturalist Gysbert van der Horst, who practised in the Roman
hospital of Santa Maria della Consolazione, kept serpents in the

hospital garden. He was an expert on fish, snakes, poisons and antidotes. As he exchanged information about fish with both Belon and Rondelet, it is possible that Aldrovandi might have met him in 1550.[4]

Medicine was the discipline that Aldrovandi had begun to study in Padua before the unfortunate Roman intermezzo, and to which he returned once he was free to go back to Bologna. He graduated in philosophy and medicine there in 1553. Though he never practised as a physician – a lack of experience that was later held against him in his dispute with the College of Physicians in Bologna in the 1570s – he continued to anatomize, still driven by that thirst for knowledge. After Giovanni Lippi, a correspondent from Arezzo, had mistakenly addressed a letter to Aldrovandi as 'professor of medicine', he later corrected his mistake and addressed him as 'professor of philosophy', but went on to assert that, whether professor or not, the appellation was not misplaced.[5]

THE MONTE BALDO CLUB

From 1551 onwards, Aldrovandi began to organize summer bot-anizing expeditions, though unlike the adventurous trip of his youth to Spain, these annual undertakings were mainly confined to the central regions around Bologna and the Marche, extending to Venice, Ravenna, Rimini and Ancona on the Adriatic coast, Livorno and Elba in the west, and Trent and Verona in the north. The claim in his later memoir written for Giacomo Boncompagni that he had seen with his own eyes 'not only the whole of Italy, but the whole of France and Spain and part of Germany' is a gross exaggeration.[6] As we saw in the previous chapter, his single trip to France and Spain was very limited in scope, and in the direction of Germany he probably never went beyond the mountains around Trent in northern Italy. Indeed, in 1554 fellow physician and nat-uralist Pietro Andrea Mattioli wrote to him urging him to travel as widely as possible while he was still young; Mattioli was more than twenty years older than the young Bolognese naturalist and complained that he was 'no longer able to go to the mountains or valleys'.[7] Only a few years later, he expressed his envy at the expeditions that Aldrovandi was able to conduct in the company of such learned scholars:

> Now that I am old and it would have been tiring for me to climb the mountains on foot, I would have infinite pleasure in remaining at the foot of the mountains to guard the horses and to do the cooking, waiting for the return of the companions to be able to see the spoils brought back from such rugged alps and mountains.[8]

He expressed a profound admiration for Aldrovandi, which meant a lot coming from a botanist who had accused Luigi Anguillara's students in Padua of not being able to tell the difference between a basil and a lettuce.[9]

It was in 1551 that Aldrovandi struck up a friendship with Luca Ghini, who taught in Pisa but used to spend the summer months botanizing in the surroundings of Bologna. Though the study of plants formed a part of the study of medicine in the universities, in 1539 Ghini became the first professor of simples in the University of Bologna, which opened up the prospect of extending field explorations to include plants that did not have any particular therapeutic value. Five years later he was appointed head of the botanical garden in Pisa, the first of its kind in Europe.[10] This was also the decade in which the first collections of dried plants or herbaria were created in central Italy, among them that of Ghini. Mention should also be made of the botanizing expeditions in Trent of Girolamo Fracastoro, Juan Páez de Castro and Diego Hurtado de Mendoza, a member of the imperial delegation to the Council of Trent, in the second half of the 1540s, which played a part in the creation of the herbarium of 950 dried plants now in the library of the Convento de San Lorenzo de El Escorial.[11] A letter addressed to Aldrovandi from late 1553 reveals that Ghini had sent seeds to Pietro Andrea Mattioli and to the Venetian nobleman Pier'Antonio Michiel, while to Aldrovandi himself he sent two lumps of alum from Bartolomeo Maranta, who was to become one of Aldrovandi's correspondents.[12] Ghini mentions that he is unable to satisfy all of Aldrovandi's requests for (dried) plants: although he once had more than six hundred, he was now only able to get his hands on fewer than half of them. Still, we can gain some idea of his herbarium from another that is still extant: the one created by a pupil of Ghini and his successor as prefect of the garden in Pisa, Andrea Cesalpino, which contains 768 exemplars along with their names in Latin, Italian and sometimes Greek.

The most famous of the locations in which both Ghini and Aldrovandi went botanizing was Monte Baldo near Verona, overlooking Lake Garda (illus. 6). It had been celebrated since the fifteenth century for the richness of its medicinal plants, and is just as well known for its rare plants among botanists today.[13] Aldrovandi was one of the group – Luigi Anguillara, prefect of the botanical garden in Padua since 1546, the physician Andrea Alpago, the Veronese apothecary Francesco Calzolari and the Veronese nobleman Gentile della Torre – who scaled Monte Baldo (2,218 metres/7,277 ft at its highest point) in June 1554.

Luigi Anguillara had already engaged in botanical fieldwork in the 1530s and claimed to have felt a burning desire to find out about plants from his early youth. He had travelled extensively, not only in Italy but in France and the lands bordering the eastern coast of the Mediterranean, though it is not known whether he ever created a collection of dried plants.

Francesco Calzolari knew Monte Baldo like the back of his hand. He worked in the family dispensary in Verona, where – as

he wrote in the dedicatory preface to his account of the journey to Monte Baldo – 'from boyhood I was involved in the family business and practice, and still am continuously very busy in that, rather than in contemplation.' But whenever he had the opportunity he took off to the mountains, which contained 'an abundance of the most beautiful and rare plants to be found, not only in Italy, but perhaps in the whole of Europe'.[14] Those expeditions afforded him a welcome break from his work in the dispensary, and he regretted that he had to cancel a planned herborizing expedition in the mountains in the summer of 1558 because the outbreak of a typhus fever epidemic kept him busy in Verona.[15] As he wrote at the end of that lyrical account interspersed with prosaic lists of more than three hundred plants, 'it is one thing to find a plant at the apothecary's, but it is another to search for it in the countryside, where their names are not written on the outside of the drawers.'[16]

In a letter dated 25 July 1554 – the first of the 39 extant letters from Calzolari to Aldrovandi, though there must have been many more – the apothecary thanks him for the gift of 25 simples received after the expedition to Monte Baldo. Only a few days later, he asks Aldrovandi what he could send him in

6 Monte Baldo (2,218 m/7,277 ft), a favourite haunt of botanists then and now.

return. This two-way exchange was actually a three-way one, because Calzolari thanks Aldrovandi on behalf of the nobleman Gentile della Torre and proposes an exchange of plants and seeds between all three of them.[17] A letter from Gentile in the same month in reply to one from Aldrovandi states that he will send him 'those things requested in that letter' as soon as possible, so the three-way exchange was already under way by then.[18]

Unlike Calzolari, Gentile della Torre came from a powerful aristocratic local family with villas scattered over the Veronese territory, many of them furnished with rustic grottos carved in the tuff of the terrain. Aldrovandi visited his 'extraordinary garden' in Verona (now the Villa Algarotti-Francescatti near the famous Giusti garden on the eastern side of the River Adige) in the same year. In a manuscript, 'Historia de coronis', written much later, Aldrovandi recalled the names of his companions during the ascent of Monte Baldo 'where I was for eight days, and we lodged in certain places of Count Gentile'.[19]

Three features of these early years of Aldrovandi's botanical fieldwork are particularly significant. While Mattioli did not keep a herbarium, 'always satisfying myself with the garden of nature and with what I have had engraved in the book', from the start Aldrovandi deliberately conformed to the new practice of collecting plants, drying them and preserving them in albums.[20] He returned from that first 1554 expedition with plants to fill the first two volumes of his herbarium. As far as we know, this was the first step that Aldrovandi took towards the formation of a collection of any kind. Calzolari wrote to Aldrovandi that he had heard about his 'very big books' from a law student called Paolo from Bologna, and hoped that Aldrovandi would spare some plants to put in his own 'book' – in both cases the reference is clearly to a herbarium, not a manuscript or planned publication.[21] The collecting pace decreased over time: if Aldrovandi had dried 4,300 plants by 1567, he was only to add another seven hundred in the next six years.[22] Although he would write and publish on so many different aspects of the natural world, botany was the one science that he passed over in his printed works. Either he felt the task was beyond him or he preferred the evidence of his herbaria, backed up in some cases by (coloured) drawings of the plants in question.

We might compare the case of the Venetian nobleman Pier'Antonio Michiel, expert advisor to the first director of the botanical garden in Padua. By 1570, when he had collected more than a thousand coloured drawings of plants in five volumes, Michiel expressed the wish to have the work printed under the auspices of the Venetian noblewoman Vincenza Loredana Marcello-Mocenigo, whose husband had been elected Doge in that same year. Vincenza, herself a student of botany, had studied under the supervision of Melchiorre Guilandino in Padua and had a botanical garden on the Venetian island of Giudecca.[23] However, it is difficult to imagine a printed book based on a quantity of drawings that, in their present form, show such a diversity of style and quality. Aldrovandi must have faced a similar unsurmountable difficulty.

This brings us to the second feature of these early years: the use of images. A letter from Luca Ghini to Aldrovandi of April 1554 refers to painted drawings that Aldrovandi had sent him, requesting him to compare them with the images in the recent publication of the commentary by Mattioli on the compendium on herbal medicine compiled by the first-century Greek physician Dioscorides.[24] In the same year Mattioli offered to send Aldrovandi images of various plants taken from the book of a Polish physician 'who assured me that he had taken them from the living plants'.[25] Mattioli had been able to inspect this painted herbarium in Trent in 1538, where he was working as a physician for Prince Bishop Bernardo Cles, who shared his interest in botany and floriculture, and carried out extensive field trips in the region.[26] Both Ghini and Aldrovandi thereby demonstrate an awareness of the fact that proper plant identification cannot depend on the written text alone but must be accompanied by an image to show the plant's morphology. After all, Bartolomeo Maranta's 1559 publication in Latin on medicinal plants and their uses was also accompanied by illustrations. Given Maranta's interest in the search for an antidote to counteract the effects of poison, it was important not to get the plant identification wrong!

Third, as the correspondence with Calzolari and della Torre makes clear, Aldrovandi was already aware that, if he were to expand his collection with plants from further afield, or even from abroad, he would have to either travel incessantly or rely on what he could obtain from contacts elsewhere. These contacts may have been collectors themselves, or mediators expected to negotiate with the collectors on Aldrovandi's behalf to get what he wanted. Given his limited means at this time, the travel option must have been out of the question, so too that of trying to rival the collections of antiquities that he had seen in Rome. However, requesting samples of live or dried plants and images of them was within his reach. By 1583 he claimed to have a total of 7,000 plants, either dried and preserved in separate volumes or represented in painted images.

Luca Ghini played an important part in the web of contacts with its epicentre in Bologna that Aldrovandi was deftly weaving in these mid-century years. In July 1554 Gentile della Torre thanked Aldrovandi for recommending him to 'the excellent physician' Luca Ghini, and only a month later he reminded Aldrovandi that his gardens were in need of 'something rare'.[27] In 1555 Calzolari thanked Aldrovandi because it was through his mediation that Luca Ghini had decided to send him a book of simples.[28] Ghini had also sent seeds from Monte Baldo to della Torre in the previous year. Clearly, the ascent of the mountain had been a bonding experience for all of them.

The 1550s were marked by a wave of publications on natural history, some of them by the naturalists whom Aldrovandi had met in Rome. Pierre Belon, who had travelled extensively in the Middle East in the entourage of the French ambassador to the court of the Turkish sultan before arriving in Rome, published an illustrated natural history of fish and another of birds in French, both in 1555. These appeared three years before the publication of another illustrated work on fish, also in French, by Guillaume Rondelet. Belon had already published an account of his observations in the Levant, including descriptions of plants and animals to be found there; he even included an account and illustration of the American armadillo (illus. 7), which is strangely out of place in the Middle East, because he had seen it in a Turkish market in Constantinople.[29] Another traveller who had been in the Middle East in the entourage of the ambassador, André Thevet, published a work in French on his travels there in 1554, and went on to publish a work on the natural history of Brazil, where he had spent ten weeks, in 1557–8. Some of the woodcuts of animals in the latter served as models for the needlework of Mary, Queen of Scots, as

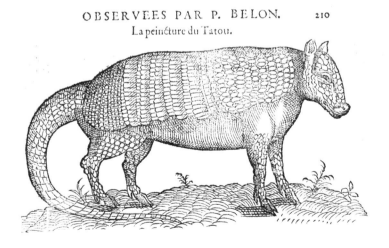

OBSERVEES PAR P. BELON.   210
La peincture du Tatou.

7 Armadillo seen in the Constantinople market, from Pierre Belon,
Les Observations de plusieurs singularitez . . . (1553).

she whiled away her years in captivity,[30] while the information about Brazilian flora was accepted and repeated by French botanists down to the eighteenth century. A shark's tooth (*glossopetra*, illus. 8) that Thevet sent to Conrad Gessner was inserted in the latter's *Historia animalium* with due acknowledgement that he had received it from the French traveller, but when Aldrovandi came to repeat the image in his *Musaeum metallicum*, he attributed it to Gessner without any mention of Thevet (MM, p. 603).[31]

The decision of these travellers to write in a simple, straightforward style in the vernacular was a novelty aimed at a lay audience, and was a feature they shared with earlier works on plants such as the *Kreuterbuch* of Hieronymus Bock, first published in 1536 but without illustrations until 1546, or the illustrated herbal of Leonhart Fuchs, whose 1532 edition in Latin was followed by a German edition the following year. When it came to works on medicinal plants, there was often a divide between the apothecaries who preferred the vernacular and the humanists who favoured the use of Latin as a mark of learning, but the distinction was by no means rigid. Writing to Aldrovandi after the latter's study trip conducted in October 1571, the apothecary

8 Shark's tooth, from Aldrovandi, *Musaeum metallicum in libros III distributum* (1648).

Calzolari expressed the hope that Aldrovandi would write the account of his journey in Italian.[32] But when the Florentine naturalist Benedetto Varchi had intended to write a sonnet dedicated to Aldrovandi after the ascent of Monte Baldo, he did not know whether it should be in Latin, Tuscan or both.[33] The Swiss naturalist Conrad Gessner wrote to his friend Johannes Kentmann in 1555 that he planned to publish a history of plants, and he corresponded with Calzolari and Aldrovandi in the hope of obtaining information about and images of plants that had not appeared in previous printed editions.[34] This project did not materialize during his lifetime, but from 1551 Gessner did embark on a long series of publications on the natural world – quadrupeds, birds, marine animals, minerals and more – which were in Latin, though abridged vernacular editions of most of them followed in due course. The eccentric French ceramicist Bernard Palissy, collector of minerals and author of a treatise on pruning and the use of fertilizer, as well as a description of a garden and a fortified town, deliberately wrote his *Recepte véritable* (1563) in French in line with his Calvinist leanings. He was not the only one: the use of the vernacular in these editions produced north of the Alps was often, but by no means always, related to the religious reform movement there.

The appearance of illustrated works marked a new stage in natural history publishing. When Paolo Giovio's treatise on Roman fish had appeared in Latin, it lacked illustrations, but the broadening of geographical horizons characteristic of the sixteenth century called for a more secure form of identification, especially of new and unknown species from outside Europe, by means of image as well as text. In the circle of Aldrovandi, the shift from Latin to a vernacular translation was reversed in the case of Mattioli, whose commentaries on Dioscorides first appeared in Italian in 1544, while the Latin edition published ten years later included 562 woodcut illustrations. In the Iberian peninsula, Andrés Laguna published a Spanish-language work largely based on Mattioli's vernacular edition and included almost all his woodcuts in the edition printed in the Spanish Habsburg city of Antwerp in 1555.

A further trait common to these new treatises was the claim to knowledge based on first-hand observation. No longer content to carry on repeating what Aristotle, Dioscorides and others had written, these writers wanted information gathered fresh in the field and especially of the latest discoveries overseas. Melchiorre Guilandino, the German-born second prefect of the botanical garden in Padua and sworn enemy of Mattioli, travelled in the Middle East and the Far East before taking up his appointment in 1561 as the successor to Luigi Anguillara. In a letter to Aldrovandi of 19 September of that year, he wrote that he had set out from Europe 'not to dispute with Pliny and Dioscorides but with the whole of antiquity together'. He planned to write a new *Naturalis historia*, but one based solely on observation carried out in his own person or by a reliable eyewitness. Disaster struck him on several occasions, and when he eventually returned to Europe in 1561 it was with empty hands.[35]

When these naturalists received images, they wanted the assurance that they had been done from life, though the phrase could carry various meanings at this time, including copies of images that had been done from life. The actual plants could be preserved in dried form, it is true, but they lost their shape and colour when flattened between successive folios, while a painted image, or failing that a hand-coloured print, could convey so much more.

The activities not only of collecting and exchanging plants but of publishing illustrated works on them were thus in the air in the 1550s. Nor was this interest confined to plants, for we know that in this decade Aldrovandi was already borrowing a collection of drawings of fish from the Venetian patriarch Daniele Barbaro and copying some of them, as well as a list of fish names

9 *Orbis stellatus* (starry pufferfish), from Aldrovandi, *Tavole*, Biblioteca
Universitaria Bologna.
10 *Mola laciniata* (sunfish), from Aldrovandi, *Tavole*, Biblioteca
Universitaria Bologna.

(illus. 9 and 10).[36] A letter from 1555 confirms that the erudite
Flaminio Nobili from Lucca was planning to send Aldrovandi
some of the fish that his father had collected.[37] In the following
year a pupil of Luca Ghini, Reiner Solenander, wrote to Aldrovandi
from Lucca to tell him that he had prepared a box of fish, shells
and zoophytes to send him. At the same time, he informed him
that he had received news from Ippolito Salviani in Rome that
the latter's book on fish was about to go to press.[38] This letter is
probably what stimulated Aldrovandi to write to Salviani pro-
posing a friendship – that is, a relation of reciprocity – between
them. The two naturalists were linked through the fact that
Salviani too had borrowed and used some of the drawings in
Barbaro's collection.[39] Although Aldrovandi's plant activities
were not destined to lead to a publication in print, his study of
fish was eventually to result in the (posthumous) publication of
De piscibus libri V in Bologna in 1613.

STATUS AND PATRONAGE

At the end of 1554 Aldrovandi began to teach logic at the University
of Bologna. In the following year he contributed to the appointment of Luca Ghini to the chair of practical medicine, a discipline
that had been introduced in the university by Mondino de' Luzzi
back in 1308, while he himself was assigned the task of teaching
filosofia straordinaria. With the death of Ghini in May 1556, this network was widened further still when Aldrovandi was appointed
professor of simples and became Ghini's natural successor within
the network of natural scientists that he and others had built up
over the years. As Calzolari reminded Aldrovandi (as he prodded
the latter to be introduced to Mattioli), it is necessary to have
friends and experience here, there and everywhere in order to
achieve perfection by learning from one another, for 'without
the help of friends it is impossible to do anything good.'[40] Not

all those who hoped for a two-way exchange with Aldrovandi were successful. At least, a certain Giovanni Fideli complained ruefully in 1556 that he had been to Bologna to collect the seeds and fruit promised him by Aldrovandi during an earlier visit, but that Aldrovandi's servant had reported that his master was out of town and left Fideli to return empty-handed. Several of Aldrovandi's correspondents complained at his slowness to respond to their letters or requests. Whether this was attributable to the state of postal services at the time or to negligence on Aldrovandi's part cannot be determined.

Aldrovandi's academic career proceeded apace in the decade of the 1550s. From professor of *filosofia straordinaria* he was promoted to that of *filosofia ordinaria* in 1559, a change in status rather than in subject-matter, since a chair in *filosofia ordinaria* was more prestigious than in its *straordinaria* counterpart. The difference was well brought out in the following year, when his students in Bologna demanded that the course he gave on simples should be upgraded from extraordinary to ordinary because of its extreme utility. Their petition was successful, and the subject-matter of what now became the ordinary course on simples was widened to include minerals and animals as well as plants.

So by the end of the 1550s Aldrovandi had secured an established position at the University of Bologna and created a network woven around what we might call the Monte Baldo club of like-minded individuals from central Italy. In a letter whose fawning tone is motivated by its writer's eagerness to obtain high-quality pharmaceutical ingredients from Aldrovandi in Bologna, where a better theriac was produced than elsewhere, Reiner Solenander stated that, after the death of Luca Ghini, he valued the opinion of Aldrovandi more highly than that of Mattioli or anyone else.[41]

Yet if Aldrovandi could represent a figure of stature for these correspondents from central Italy, he must already have been thinking of casting his net further afield. In a letter to him written

at the end of 1552, Luca Ghini noted that the correspondence
was being conveyed to Aldrovandi in the hands of Gervasio
Mastarell, a French student of Rondelet who had botanized in
Spain.[42] In recommending him to Aldrovandi, Ghini will have
been aware that he was opening up to the Bolognese scientist the
possibility of drawing on fieldwork conducted beyond the confines
of the Italian border. For instance, we find a reference to the dried
branch and fruit of an American tree (*Persea*) taken from the only
exemplar in Europe known to Aldrovandi at the time, which he
received from a contact in Valencia around 1568.[43] At one point
he summed up the locations of the suppliers of his images of
plants, animals and minerals as including 'Genoa, Venice, Padua,
Florence, Rome, Naples, Rimini, Bohemia, Germany, Spain,
Bavaria and Ingolstadt, Constantinople, Nuremberg, Paris, Madrid,
Portugal and Lisbon'.[44]

Besides this desire to move outwards, Aldrovandi's ambition
drove him to seek satisfaction in an upward direction. In a letter
of 1576, Aldrovandi looked back on a moment that occurred
fourteen or fifteen years earlier, when – he claimed – the Grand
Duke of Florence, Cosimo I, had invited him 'to go to Pisa to teach
the history of plants and natural things, and ever since I have
been greatly indebted to this House of Medici for so many reasons'.[45] In 1543 Cosimo had successfully convinced Luca Ghini
to move from Bologna to Pisa, where preparations were going
ahead to establish the first botanical garden in Europe, but in
1560 Aldrovandi decided to stay in Bologna with its highly prestigious university, and where he had already proposed to the
Senate the establishment of a botanical garden modelled on the
Pisan one. Perhaps he was also put off by the bad reputation of
the Pisan food, soil, air and water, as his friend Gabriele Falloppia
complained.[46] In the following decade, however, Cardinal
Ferdinando de' Medici wrote to his brother Francesco recommending 'Doctor Ulisse Aldrovandi, Bolognese gentleman, for

the Studio of Pisa', initiating a correspondence that was to continue for almost thirty years.[47]

Within the pyramidal hierarchy that characterized Italian princely courts down to the end of the *ancien régime*, there was nothing shameful about setting one's sights on securing assistance from that quarter. Any ambitious scientist who did not have private means or some richly endowed ecclesiastical function was bound to seek patronage higher up. In the case of a naturalist, unless he could permit himself unlimited travel abroad, the only means of gaining access to non-local plants and animals was through the concentration of these objects in the courts thanks to their widespread exchange networks and the long-standing tradition of princely gifts.[48] An example of this is the menagerie with lions, leopards, monkeys, civet cats and bears installed in the Vatican by Pope Leo X, who was even given a famous Indian elephant as a gift from King Manuel of Portugal in 1514. The immortalization of this elephant in drawings and even a fountain is tangible evidence of the ability of such well-endowed persons to disseminate knowledge of their possessions beyond the confines of their own court.[49] So if a naturalist like Aldrovandi would be able to tap into such a rich source of knowledge about the natural world, there was nothing inherently fawning about his quest for patronage. After Charles de l'Écluse had been appointed by Maximilian II in Vienna to superintend his gardens in 1573, Aldrovandi wrote to the Flemish botanist to congratulate him and to send him 86 seeds of various sorts to plant in the diverse terrains within the boundary of the extensive gardens. Never wanting to miss any opportunity to obtain patronage among the high-ranking and wealthy, he concluded the letter with the hope that Clusius would show the seeds and recommend him to the emperor.[50]

Aldrovandi's correspondence with Mattioli, who had written to him about the munificence of his Habsburg patron in Prague in paying the highly skilled painter Giorgio Liberale to produce

coloured images of animals and plants, shows that Aldrovandi
was already enquiring about the possibility of gaining princely
patronage elsewhere in 1557.[51] Moreover, if he planned to publish
his findings, having a powerful patron would help to protect the
author against plagiarists. Such patronage could also be a means
of (re)confirming a naturalist's status, as the dispute on theriac
will show.

THE IMPORTANCE OF THERIAC

Around the middle of the sixteenth century, Giovanni Odorico
Melchiori, a correspondent of Aldrovandi, sent Mattioli a description, illustration and dried specimen of a plant called scurzonera,
which he had obtained from a Catalan doctor in Spain and was
supposed to be a strong antidote against snakebite. Concerns
about how to treat snakebite, however, were much older. Already
in the first century BC, a certain Crateuas, a Greek physician who
is credited with having produced the first illustrated herbal,
developed a method of elaborating an antidote against all poisons. He was in the service of the ruler of Pontus (the stretch of
land on the east coast of the Black Sea in what is now Turkey),
Mithridates VI, who was also interested in pharmacology and was
terrified of being poisoned by his enemies: hence the antidote
was called mithridate. After the defeat of the Pontine ruler at the
hands of the Roman general Pompey in AD 63, the secret passed
into Roman hands, and Andromachus, a Cretan physician of Nero,
wrote it down in a 174-line poem in Greek.

The Roman version was not identical to the Greek formula,
as not all of the ingredients were readily available everywhere.
The new antidote known as theriac, which was considered even
more effective than mithridate, was composed of no fewer than
64 animal, plant and mineral ingredients. That the number 64
is the product of $4 \times 4 \times 4$ is significant in view of Galen's theory

of the four humours and their correspondence with the four seasons, the four cardinal points and so on. Problems could arise in trying to produce this composite because not every substitute was as effective as the original simple, or required a modification of the dosage, or had to be prepared in a different way. This was no obstacle to the successful reputation of theriac, which found in Galen its most eloquent promoter – if it was ineffective, this must have been due to recourse to an improper succedaneum or substitute, improper dosage, or a modification in its preparation and/or storage conditions.

Especially after the Black Death of the fourteenth century and the outbreaks of the plague that followed, interest in the possibility of an antidote that would be effective against all ailments continued unabated. In the sixteenth century, naturalists and herbalists turned their attention to the health (and financial) benefits to be derived from the preparation of a successful antidote.[52] One of these was Bartolomeo Maranta. He had studied botany with Luca Ghini in Pisa and was by now a member of the College of Physicians of the prestigious University of Salerno. Though the work is credited only to Maranta, the *Della theriaca et del mithridato*, published in Naples in 1572, was actually co-written with Ferrante Imperato, one of the eight members of the supervisory body (*Protomedicato*) whose task it was to guarantee the standards and procedures applied by the apothecaries in Naples.

The collaboration was between two men, each of whose expertise complemented that of the other: while Imperato was experienced in obtaining the necessary ingredients and in their elaboration for medicinal purposes, Maranta saw his role more as the humanist theoretician whose authority was required to confer credibility on the publication. In fact, in the dedication of the work to Imperato, he compared his own role with that of the architect, while his colleague's was more like that of the master builder.

The relation between Maranta and Imperato mirrors the one that was growing between Aldrovandi and Calzolari, as the correspondence illustrates. Already in the first extant letter from Calzolari, the Veronese apothecary expresses the hope that knowledge of the succcedanei successfully employed by Aldrovandi will enable him to perfect the theriac on which he is working; the tragacanthus that he mentions in the same letter was an important ingredient in theriac but difficult to find in Europe. In November 1555 Calzolari repeated his request for news of any new books on simples and of the succedanei in Bologna. Three years later he was still eager to obtain 'a copy of the theriac made in Bologna and a copy of the succedanei used in it', a need that had become all the more pressing in view of an epidemic that had broken out in Verona in the summer of 1558.[53] By 1566 Calzolari was able to publish a defence of his theriac, which had earned the approval of the College of Physicians in Verona, seconded by Aldrovandi. With this cover by both the physicians and the naturalists, Calzolari even exhibited the ingredients of his theriac in a special room in his museum to demonstrate their purity.

In Lucca, where a College of Physicians was established in 1563 modelled on that of Bologna, one of its members, Gregorio Cantarini, wrote to Aldrovandi in March 1564 asking for a list of the succedanei that had been approved by the corresponding Bolognese body.[54] In the same town, Reiner Solenander was also trying to compose the theriac whose composition had been described by Andromachus. In a long letter to Aldrovandi he asked for information about a number of succedanei: whether he could use *apio hortense* instead of *petroselino* (presumably celery instead of parsley, though these are imprecise terms), about the best type of *terra lemnia* and so on, including a list of succedanei that he had received from Naples and on which he would like to hear Aldrovandi's opinion.[55] In the following decade, another correspondent

of Aldrovandi from Lucca, Giovanni Battista Fulcheri, was also
engaged in preparing theriac. In October 1569 he sent Aldrovandi
a sample of his theriac along with a flask of orange blossom oil,
and in the spring of 1571 he wrote: 'I have killed a number of vipers
to make theriac, and if you know the best place for that, I would
be grateful to hear it.' Another of Aldrovandi's correspondents,
Ferrante Imperato, provided Fulcheri with various sorts of alum
in 1572, the year in which the Neapolitan apothecary's work on
theriac was published.[56]

One of the most important differences between the ingredients of Andromachus' theriac and the mithridate of Crateuas
was that in the Roman version a scaly lizard found in North
Africa was replaced by the viper's venom that was more readily
available in Rome and Italy. It was the use of vipers in theriac that
brought matters to a head in a bitter dispute involving Aldrovandi's
theriac which led to another visit to Rome, this time in 1577.

The appointment of Aldrovandi as one of the medical super-
visors of Bologna in 1574 triggered a dispute with the local
physicians, since he was not a practising physician and had come
in for criticism for progressively abandoning the teaching of medicine for the study of simples. Regional rivalry played a part too,
as is shown by a letter from the Bolognese physician Girolamo
Donino of 1560, in which he appealed to Aldrovandi's solidarity
with a fellow native of Bologna because 'all the physicians involved
in the dispute are Pisan doctors.'[57] A critical stage was reached in
1575, a jubilee year, when the physicians and apothecaries of
Bologna joined forces to make a special theriac to commemorate
the occasion. This was a direct challenge to Aldrovandi's bold
claim to have made not only the best theriac, but one that was an
improvement on the ancient Galenic formula. The dice, however,
were loaded against them, for Ugo Boncompagni, elected to the
papal throne as Pope Gregory XIII in May 1572, was a cousin of
Aldrovandi's mother, Veronica Marescalchi. The papal legate

intervened in the dispute and forbade the sale of the jubilee theriac. Aldrovandi's rather weak standing as a medical authority would not have saved his reputation, but papal intervention did.

Nevertheless, the affair did not die down, and eventually the papal legate passed the case on to Rome. Thus, once again, as in 1550, Aldrovandi found himself in Rome as a result of a local dispute in Bologna. By now, however, his chances of success were much higher; a contemporary characterized the papal court as one in which 'they are all Bolognese and pass the ball to one another.'[58] Besides Aldrovandi's family ties with the pope, the reputation that he had built up in the field of *materia medica* was a strong card in his favour. In May 1577 the Bolognese Pope Gregory XIII issued a papal bull demanding that Aldrovandi be reinstated to his full honours and position. Aldrovandi regained his position in the College of Physicians and as director of the botanical garden in Bologna, a role that he had held since its institution in 1568, and obtained a promise of financial assistance with the publication of his manuscripts. Within the space of 25 years, he had managed to secure his standing as a leading naturalist in Italy. But he had set his sights further afield.

THREE

Forming a Collection, Friendship and Patronage

he beginnings of Aldrovandi's collection probably go back to the months spent in Rome in 1549–50 and their immediate aftermath, when he began to form the collection of dried plants that would eventually run to fifteen volumes, as well as minerals and fish. That collection had the same dual purpose: it was a status object and it was a study collection for his own personal use and that of his colleagues who were granted access to its wealth of materials.

Seeds, roots and dried plants presented few practical problems for a collector like Aldrovandi as they were small and easy to store, but their actual collection could present more problems due to the seasonal and meteorological conditions. The hot and dry summer of 1572 depleted three-quarters of the stock of the garden of Giovanni Battista Fulcheri in Lucca, where further havoc was caused by the cold of the ensuing winter, and the following spring the incessant rains prevented him from sending any plants.[1] In Rimini, the antiquarian, physician and naturalist Costanzo Felici wrote to Aldrovandi that the winter of 1566–7 had destroyed many rare plants, and he was unable to send paintings of them because after the garden owner's death, he was unable to lay his hands on them.[2] In Florence, Stefano Rosselli reported the damage to plants and trees from a hailstorm in the winter of 1567–8, while the following year it was storms and rains that prevented him from going out of town to collect plants for

Aldrovandi.[3] Calzolari in Verona met with a multitude of mis-
fortunes in one year: the death of his wife, a big storm, and the
theft of more than a thousand ducats at the hands of eight masked
highwaymen prevented him from supplying Joachim Camerarius
in Nuremberg with all that he had requested.[4] In Venice, cats
destroyed the fishes Pier'Antonio Michiel had put out to dry in
1560, and six years earlier Mattioli had complained to Aldrovandi
that the roots of two 'beans' of elephant ears (*Colocasia*) he had
been given by a Polish physician and planted were eaten while
they were still young, leading to their exsiccation.[5] More dramatic
was the earthquake of 1570 that shook Ferrara, destroying 40
per cent of the buildings in the city and prompting Pirro Ligorio
to design the first anti-seismic structure. The duke, who had

Garulus Bohemicus mas noster qui apparuit anno 1570.

11 Bohemian waxwing, from Aldrovandi, *Tavole*, Biblioteca Universitaria
Bologna.

designated three gardens for rare plants, had allocated two rooms in his castello to a physician and friend of Aldrovandi, Alfonso Pancio, to house his collection of *naturalia*. Both rooms fell to the ground and the castello was rendered uninhabitable.[6] But 1570 was a positive year, too: on a painting of a Bohemian waxwing, a bird not normally found in Italy, is written the date 1570 to mark one of the unusual appearances of the 'Garulus Bohemicus' in the peninsula in that year (illus. 11).[7]

Once the difficulties of collection had been overcome, there were those of transport to contend with. The transportation of plants and seeds was relatively easy provided due care was taken in packaging them. As the dates of the correspondence between Ippolito Salviani and Aldrovandi show, the best time of the year for sending plants was the spring, before the hot days of the summer began. Writing from Verona in 1554, Calzolari asked Aldrovandi to send him plants 'in boxes with soil and securely tied' via the address of an intermediary in Venice, the apothecary Pierantonio Danzo.[8] Given the perishability of these materials, proper co-ordination was required. Thus, to send plants from Verona to Bologna without the risk of their rotting on the way, Aldrovandi was requested in 1557 to inform Calzolari when to dispatch them to Venice so that his contact there, the printer Vincenzo Valgrisi, could send them on to Aldrovandi without delay.[9] There are many complaints, whether feigned or genuine, on the part of Aldrovandi's correspondents that they have been unable to send him more because of the impatience of the carriers. Fulcheri went up the San Giuliano mountain to botanize in 1573, but by the time he returned to Lucca he found that the carriers had already left, despite their promises to wait for him.[10] Zoological specimens were also prone to damage of a different kind: just as Aldrovandi was completing the first volume of his work on ornithology, Fulcheri could only send him the head, foot and tibia of a bird that he called a marsh eagle, as locals from Lucca had eaten the rest. Aldrovandi duly recorded the fact right at the end of the first volume, and though he was unable to determine the exact nature of the bird, he included its beak among the collection of beaks in his museum (ORN, I, p. 891).

Some idea of the extent of these networks of friends can be gauged from a letter sent to Aldrovandi in 1572 by Pompeo Mattioli, nephew of the famous Pietro Andrea Mattioli whose works Valgrisi had printed. From Siena Pompeo had ordered a parcel to be dispatched to a gentleman in Florence, where it was delayed in customs, to be forwarded to the brother of Valgrisi in Venice, who was in turn to pass it on to Vincenzo, who would then ensure its dispatch to Pietro Andrea, who was in the service of the Habsburg Archduke Ferdinand in Prague at the time.[11]

Seeds could also be tried out to see what grew from them. In one of his earliest letters to the Grand Duke of Tuscany, Francesco de' Medici, containing a description of four coloured drawings of American trees that Aldrovandi sent to Francesco, he mentions that 'these truly are plants whose seeds it would be worth having to multiply this science of the knowledge of plants.'[12] Another rarity, this one from the East, was the tulip. The first known tulips in Europe were flowering in the gardens of a happy few around 1560 (Pier'Antonio Michiel sent a yellow one to Aldrovandi in 1559).[13] This was long before the famous tulip craze of the 1630s, so when Francesco Calzolari expressed the hope of obtaining some tulip seeds from Aldrovandi in 1572 he was aiming high.[14]

Aldrovandi's friendship with Fulcheri, who had a celebrated garden in Lucca, began in 1565 when the apothecary visited Bologna with the gift of a 'book of simples coloured naturally'.[15] Two years later Aldrovandi received a box from Fulcheri that contained a fava bean, a chestnut and a 'bean of India' that the latter had promised in their 1565 meeting to send to him. This was followed by 'a packet of dried herbs' that Fulcheri had received from the naturalist Jacques Reynaud in Marseille.[16] In the course of the following years he provided Aldrovandi with oriental hyacinth bulbs, the roots of supposed hermodactyls (used as a cathartic), samples of fragrant cedarwood and a flask of his own theriac. When he received more than a hundred sorts of seeds 'from our ambassador' in Spain, he planted them and promised to send Aldrovandi some of the plants if they germinated. He also sent him some seeds of the American sunflower and asked for his advice on the best way to plant and tend them.[17] The two friends exchanged lists of desiderata as a way of increasing their collections without unnecessary duplication, and a network stretching from Marseille to Spain was extremely valuable for a naturalist and collector whose movements were largely confined to central Italy. All the same, practical problems continually got in the way. In February 1569 Fulcheri candidly admitted that he had lost all the letters with lists of desiderata on the part of Aldrovandi in the street. Two months later, Fulcheri complained that the plants that he had received from Cesalpino were already so dried up that there was no point in forwarding them to Aldrovandi in Bologna. A month earlier, a delay in receiving a list of plants from Pisa and Lucca that Aldrovandi had requested meant that, when Fulcheri went to send him some plants, he was told that the carrier had already left. By June it had become too hot to be able to send plants; he promised to send seeds instead later in the year.[18]

Aldrovandi's attention had been drawn to Fulcheri by another correspondent from Lucca, the physician Gregorio Cantarini, who also offered to send Aldrovandi some items that he had received from Spain in 1571.[19] A decade earlier, in the summer of 1561, he begged for two or three leaves of a horseshoe vetch, fresh or dried, on behalf of a friend. When Aldrovandi replied that he had only one plant, Cantarini went on to ask him to conduct an experiment with it: he was to put an iron rod next to the plant, touching the roots and the leaves, and to leave it there overnight. Cantarini was at pains to explain that he was asking Aldrovandi to do this not out of 'incantations and fantastic fantasies', but as a scientific experiment to see whether the rod was still touching the root and leaves in the morning, or whether the plant had caused it to bend. Needless to say, a week later he wrote: 'If that plant will produce the effect that I described, I would like to have information about it; but since it did not do it after one night, nor in two or three, I do not expect any change.' Aldrovandi sent him a horseshoe vetch of his own the following year.[20]

Fish also formed part of these networks of exchange. Letters from the Neapolitan professor of philosophy at the Studio in Pisa, Simone Porzio, indicate that he was supplying Cosimo I de' Medici with rare fish from La Spezia, as well as commissioning Francesco Ubertini (Bacchiacca) to paint them, in 1549 and 1550.[21] Fish had already attracted Aldrovandi's interest in those same years during his first stay in Rome, and the broadening of his teaching on simples to include animals and minerals in 1560, as well as his acquisition of the mineral collection of Luca Ghini, will have confirmed that wider interest. There were, however, practical problems. Gregorio Cantarini promised to send Aldrovandi some minerals, a spiny lobster and a mantis shrimp from the Cinque Terre coast in October 1559, but three years later he apologized for the delay on the grounds that he was still waiting to receive a flying gurnard and other fish from La Spezia, while something had gone wrong during the drying of the fish that he had received.[22] Writing to Aldrovandi in February 1560, the fish expert Ippolito Salviani promised to send him some of the dried fish that the Bolognese naturalist had requested, but he would have to wait because they did not reach the fish market in Rome until later in the season, and some on Aldrovandi's list were never to be found in Rome at all because they lived in the rivers and lakes of northern Italy.[23]

The petrified nautilus shell and other petrifactions that Calzolari received from Mantua at the end of 1571 were easy enough to send on to Aldrovandi, and so was the box of various fish, shells and zoophytes that Reiner Solenander promised to send Aldrovandi from Lucca.[24] However, when Calzolari promised to send him a trout, a carp and other fish from Lake Garda, he had to ensure that they were properly prepared.[25] Of course, fish would lose their natural colour after only a few hours, which explains why Aldrovandi waxed lyrical about the invention of a fluid by Francesco de' Medici in which the bodies of fish could be preserved with their natural colour.[26]

Obstacles of a different kind occurred too. In March 1567 Melchiorre Guilandino wrote from Padua to Aldrovandi that he had been 'in continuous hope of being sent a hazel grouse (*francolino*) from Vicenza or Bassano to mate with my own, to the greater contentment of them both, but there is a continuing delay because of the scarcity of these birds in these places'.[27] Human nature could get in the way too: writing to Aldrovandi on Christmas Day 1571, Calzolari warned him that there was little chance of obtaining an exemplar of petrified bread from a member of the della Torre family because 'they are in the hands of important men who want to have important and rare things to complete their collection, and money is no object when it comes to obtaining rare things.'[28] This was presumably the 'petrified bread with many fissures in which mosaics can be seen' that Aldrovandi had admired that year together with a pearl-bearing oyster and a porphyry statue of Silenus in the octagonal studio of Girolamo della Torre, probably located in Via Salvatore Vecchio in the centre of Verona.[29]

Pier'Antonio Michiel cultivated both indigenous and exotic species in his garden in the Dorsoduro neighbourhood of Venice, but not everyone found it easy to gain entry. For instance, on 9 May 1554 the plant expert Antonio Compagnoni, who hoped that Aldrovandi would one day come to Venice to help him identify the fishes displayed on the market, wrote to his mentor about a visit to take some plants on Aldrovandi's behalf to Michiel: he was told to leave them there and come back some other time, and the only view that he gained of the 'little garden' was from the outside.[30] A few months later, Mattioli wrote to Aldrovandi that such behaviour was unworthy of one gentleman to another, and that Michiel should therefore be considered 'worse than an ass'.[31]

By the end of 1572 Aldrovandi realized that his hopes of an American expedition were in vain. In the previous year he had visited Calzolari's collection in Verona during a study tour that also took in Ferrara, Mantua, Vicenza, Padua and Venice, but now when he projected an expedition to explore the natural resources of a region, that region had shrunk to the size of Tuscany and the island of Elba. Henceforth he would have to make do with what he could obtain in the way of seeds, exemplars and images from exchanges with friends and colleagues elsewhere, both within the Italian peninsula and further afield.

Aldrovandi had heard about the famous garden of Jean de Brancion, a member of the Habsburg court circle in Malines, which included several American plants as well as indigenous ones, and this may have made Aldrovandi even more determined to try to set up a relation of reciprocity with him.[32] In the earliest known letter from Aldrovandi to Charles de l'Écluse, dated February 1569, he mentioned that Brancion had sent him images 'from life' of a flamingo, a black brant and a bald eagle, together with some exotic plants that Clusius had brought back from Spain and entrusted to Brancion to be passed on to Aldrovandi.[33] During Clusius' travels in the Iberian peninsula earlier in the decade, he had discovered the *Coloquios dos simples* of the Portuguese naturalist García de Orta and immediately begun to translate the work into Latin for the international community.[34] It was this work that had brought the Flemish naturalist to the attention of Aldrovandi.

In this same letter Aldrovandi thanked Clusius for his diligence in providing descriptions of those three birds for Aldrovandi's benefit, and went on to beg him to intercede with Brancion on his behalf to send him a number of seeds that he had requested 'so that I may plant them in the ground of our public garden for the benefit of my students', a reference to the new *hortus* that had been created in Bologna in 1568. The letter concludes with a request for a copy of Clusius' own observations on Iberian flora, but political troubles in the Netherlands prevented the publication of that work until 1576.[35] Aldrovandi repeated that request in a letter to Clusius from February 1570 and confirmed that the seeds had arrived and been duly planted in the *hortus*. He also repeated the hope that Clusius would share with him any unusual seed, dried plant or other item that came his way and to urge Brancion, 'who has infinite plants in his well-stocked garden', to do the same on Aldrovandi's behalf. The letters from this period are revealing of Aldrovandi's strategic use of the term 'friendship' as a means to obtain plants from the Southern Netherlands, Spain, Portugal and America without having to stir from Bologna.

Another link to America, this one among Aldrovandi's contacts in Italy, was the Tuscan physician and naturalist Michele Mercati, creator of a considerable museum of metals and fossils housed in several rooms, who was called to Rome around 1570 to create and supervise the new garden of simples in the Vatican grounds. The creation of the garden of simples was an initiative of Pope Pius v, whose interest in medicinal plants was widely known. A link between Rome and Bologna was forged when the two naturalists began to exchange seeds and plants, and for Aldrovandi it meant an indirect means of obtaining items from America. At the beginning of 1572, the papal legate in Portugal sent no fewer than 160 rare plants and flowers, probably from the Americas, to Rome as a confirmation of Philip II's promise to share them with the head of the Catholic Church.[36] In this way Mercati furnished Aldrovandi with several American plants, among them tobacco, maize, tomato and capsicum. Not all of these will have thrived in the climate of Bologna, but the Jerusalem artichoke proved to be easy to cultivate in European soil even further north in France and the Netherlands. Other plants came from the East, such as the much-coveted tulips. Besides these exchanges of objects, Mercati also proved to be a useful source of information about new and exotic arrivals in the Vatican gardens, such as the two banana plants sent from Alexandria via Sicily to Rome, where they struggled to survive owing to the city's cooler climate.[37] Pier'Antonio Michiel had also received some banana plants a decade earlier, and the German medical student Johannes Kentmann painted a banana plant in a vase that he had seen in the garden of Pietro Bembo in Padua in 1548.[38] More than forty years later, Joachim Jungermann wrote to Charles de l'Écluse about the exotic plants to be found in the garden of Pietro Bembo's son Torquato, urging him to encourage Torquato to continue to display an eagerness to acquire exotic plants, 'for I know no one in Venice or Padua who takes greater delight in them.'[39]

Still further south, in Naples, Aldrovandi could count on the support of the owner of one of the other major collections of natural history in sixteenth-century Italy, Ferrante Imperato. Like Calzolari in Verona, Imperato was an apothecary who kept a museum in the same premises as his dispensary from the mid-1560s (illus. 12), and, as we saw in the previous chapter, took up a stance in the theriac battle with the publication of *Della theriaca et del mithridato*, co-written with Bartolomeo Maranta, in 1572. Imperato and Maranta collaborated on their experiments using the materials in the former's collection. In July 1573, Imperato wrote to Aldrovandi for advice on how to tell whether or not a dissected viper was pregnant; no matter in what season he dissected them, they always had what seemed to be a thread of eggs, suggesting that they were always pregnant. The same letter accompanied the dispatch of a live lizard. Another kind of lizard ran so quickly that

it was almost impossible to capture without killing it, which had compelled Imperato to send Aldrovandi a dead exemplar preserved in honey, but now he had managed to catch one alive.[40] These living specimens were dispatched in boxes with holes for breathing and sent to Aldrovandi's brother in Rome.

Important though these connections with apothecaries and physicians in Verona, Rome and Naples were, Aldrovandi realized that he was in need of a patron with higher social standing, influence and wealth, as well as one close to his radius of operations. A person who fulfilled all these conditions was the Grand Duke of Tuscany, Francesco de' Medici, with whom Aldrovandi was to maintain very cordial relations until the ruler's death in 1587. On the one hand, becoming a client of the Grand Duke would certainly serve to enhance Aldrovandi's prestige, but besides its implications for his professional status, at a more practical level it was a way of putting him in contact with the infinite varieties of natural specimens with which he furnished his collection.

12 Museum of Ferrante Imperato, Naples, from Ferrante Imperato, *Dell'historia naturale* (1599).

MEDICI PATRONAGE

Collecting wild and exotic animals had a long tradition in Florence, going back to the gift of a leopard and other wild animals to the Commune at the end of the thirteenth century. Outside Florence the tradition was kept up in the sixteenth century by the Medici Pope Leo X, who had a menagerie in the Vatican, and by Ferdinando de' Medici's collection of lions, bears, ostriches and other wild animals in Rome before his transfer to Florence in 1588. Fifteenth-century painters increasingly depicted them, as in Benozzo Gozzoli's grand fresco wrapped around three walls of the Palazzo Medici which depicted animals familiar from the Italian countryside as well as the more exotic camels, dromedaries, leopards, cheetahs and a monkey. In the mid-sixteenth century Bacchiacca included a porcupine, donkeys, cows, a horse, a goat, a monkey, a bear, a sheep, a rabbit, red-legged partridges, camels and a woodpecker in his canvas of the *Gathering of Manna*. The grotto in the Villa Medici at Castello, one of the Medici villas on the hilltops overlooking Florence, featured sculptures of European animals and the exotic giraffe, rhinoceros, gazelle, leopard and monkey; an American turkey (illus. 13) was one of the bronze birds on the walls by Giambologna.[41] Bacchiacca also painted highly accurate depictions of plants based on live or, failing that, dried specimens copied from the herbarium of Luca Ghini on the walls of the private studiolo of Cosimo in the Palazzo Vecchio in 1545.[42] The Medici showed a keen interest in the natural world and liked to show their domination of it, as symbolized by the famous fifth-century sculpture of the chimera: when Michel de Montaigne visited Florence in 1581, he recorded the legend that the beast had been captured live in a mountain cave and brought from there, implying that the sculpture was an *ad vivum* representation.[43]

The Medici also conformed to the practice of most princely collectors in accumulating antiquities, precious stones and metals. The excavation of Etruscan antiquities in Arezzo, where the

13 Giambologna, *Turkey*, 1567, bronze.

bronze chimera had been found, served to bolster the claims of the Medici to be descendants of a noble Etruscan family and therefore worthy of the title Grand Dukes of Tuscany. Already in 1551 the theory of their Etruscan origin was published in a work by Guillaume Postel and dedicated to Cosimo I in which he attempted to derive both the Etruscan and Tuscan languages from the 'Aramaic' that he postulated was spoken by Noah and his descendants.[44] Promoted under Cosimo I and vigorously debated within the circle of the Accademia Fiorentina, this claim to Etruscan descent was continued by Francesco I, who brought the treasures accumulated by his ancestors together in the Galleria degli Uffizi, with its epicentre in the octagonal Tribuna. This move was completely in line with the concept of the princely Kunstkammer that he shared with his father, Cosimo, whose collection in the Palazzo Vecchio showed the marked taste for antiquity that was characteristic of such aristocratic treasures.

Francesco de' Medici, who became Prince Regent in 1564 and Grand Duke of Tuscany ten years later, demonstrated continuity with his predecessors in taking a lively interest in the natural world and combined both *naturalia* and *artificialia* within the same space. Between 1570 and 1575 he commissioned a small space for study (*studiolo*) and alchemistic pursuits in the Palazzo Vecchio, with Giorgio Vasari in charge of supervising the decoration. A 1574 inventory of its contents lists a large number of natural elements, such as specimens of stone and coral, as well as man-made objects such as axes and other weapons made of metal. The natural meeting place of the twin interests in *naturalia* and *artificialia* was in those objects like minerals or shells that were products of nature but could be modified or incorporated in elaborate mounts, such as the many examples of nautilus shells converted into vases or other vessels with the addition of metal stands and sometimes encrusted with jewels. Such a broadening of interests was in perfect harmony with dynastic ambitions, with the implied assumption that knowledge about the world went hand in hand with mastery of that world.[45]

It may have been the failure of Aldrovandi's attempts to gain support for an expedition to America, the Near East or even one closer to home on Crete that led him to turn to Francesco de' Medici in 1577. Besides the prospect of widening the scope of his collection of dried or dead specimens of the natural world, another important aspect of Aldrovandi's ties with the Medici court in Florence was the access that it would give him to living animals, such as the two snakes, a horned viper and a sand viper, immortalized in a painting by Jacopo Ligozzi (illus. 14). Aldrovandi's interest in the gift of the two live vipers was not purely scientific, since his victory in the 'battle of the theriac' had been secured partly on the basis of his criticism of the viper's blood used in the theriac prepared by the College of Physicians and apothecaries of Bologna. To support his claim, Aldrovandi had a viper dissected in his house and shown to an assembly of doctors and other scholars. In 1583, a year in which Aldrovandi's correspondence with Francesco is primarily concerned with plants, we learn from another source that three elks arrived in the Medici court from Sweden through the intermediary of a merchant from Lucca.[46] One of the elks, a novelty in Florence at this date, was painted by Ligozzi four years later; of the few paintings by the artist to have reached Bologna, it is the only one to be autographed (illus. 15). On another occasion, Aldrovandi recorded having seen two gazelles, a fawn and an American peccary in Bologna. His artist was able to record them there before they were taken to be presented to the Medici court.

In an appendix to his autobiography, Aldrovandi dated his visit to the Grand Duke of Tuscany in 1577, where he was well received thanks to the recommendation of Monsignor Alberto Bolognetti, a distant relative of the Bolognese pope who had been called to the papal court in Rome in the previous year.[47] Aldrovandi duly

*crastes serpens perniciosissimus ex
Lybia ad serenissimum Hetruriæ
Ducem allatus una cum Ammo-
dite: Qui mihi utrumqs uiuum
donauit, et deinde etiam ambos i
depictos ad me misit.*

congratulated Bolognetti on his promotion as papal legate to the
Florentine court in February 1576 and offered his services as a
consultant on animals, plants and minerals to the Grand Duke,
'a most discerning inquirer into the properties of natural things,
a study truly suited to his most fertile and fortunate intellect'.[48]
     Aldrovandi described that visit as follows:

> He [Francesco de' Medici] entertained Dr Aldrovandi
> for two days. On the first day he wanted to show him all
> the things kept in the Casino, where he spent three hours
> in the presence of Monsignor and many physicians that
> His Highness had summoned. He wanted to know the

14 Jacopo Ligozzi, horned viper and sand viper, from Aldrovandi, *Tavole*,
Biblioteca Universitaria Bologna.

15 Jacopo Ligozzi, *Elk*, 1587, from Aldrovandi, *Tavole*, Biblioteca
Universitaria Bologna.

opinion of Aldrovandi on all the things he was shown, having also shown him all the paintings done from life by Jacomo Ligozzi, which lack nothing but the breath of life, and asked him not to leave for Rome on the following day, but to visit his palace where he had everything methodically arranged.

He did not fail to obey His Highness and went there the next morning. For five continuous hours he showed him all the *naturalia* such as stones, jewels, soils, metals, etc., and many paintings of fish done from life. At the same time he asked Sir Gaddi to show all the ancient gold, silver and bronze coins to Giulio de Velli of Bologna, a man well versed in the study of antiquities. All around the walls of the coin cabinet were hung more than a hundred wooden panels painted with birds by my painter Master Gian Triulxi, taken from my exemplars before the Grand Duke had taken on Jacomo Ligozzi, who is a second Apelles, as can be seen from some figures sent to me by His Highness by the hand of this painter.[49]

Francesco de' Medici was in his mid-thirties and Aldrovandi some twenty years older when they met. It must have been clear to both parties where they stood: the younger man could benefit from the expertise of Aldrovandi in matters of natural history, who promised to dedicate to the Grand Duke some of his writings, 'in each of which many beautiful secrets of nature will be discovered, as well as properties arising from the form of those compounds of animate and inanimate things'.[50] In return, the Bolognese naturalist stood to gain from the advantages of Medici patronage for various purposes. Relations between the two men were cordial, based on their shared curiosity in matters of the natural world, but the due protocol of patronage was respected in the concluding salutations: while Aldrovandi signed as 'the most humble and

devoted servant of your Most Serene Highness', Francesco reciprocated with 'Your Grand Duke of Tuscany'. In one of the earliest
letters in their correspondence, dated September 1577, Aldrovandi
expressed his regret at not being able to attend the baptism of
Francesco's son (by his mistress Bianca Cappello), accompanying
his letter with 'a box with twenty-five *naturalia*' that he hoped would
be new to the Grand Duke.[51] As the accompanying catalogue provided details on each one, we know that they included the four
paintings of American trees that Aldrovandi had received from
Portugal eight years before. Though not one of the extant Mexican
objects from the Medici collections can be assigned to Francesco's
years as Grand Duke, he is known to have been at least as interested
in America as his father, Cosimo, and these paintings must have
been a particularly welcome arrival. American plants circulated
between Bologna and Florence in the following years: Aldrovandi
received an American cypress vine or quamoclit and an American
nasturtium from Francesco via the latter's gardener Giuseppe
Casabona in May 1583.[52] Later in the same year Aldrovandi was
able to show Casabona round his own private garden and the
botanical garden in Bologna, and many years later, in 1595, when
Casabona was at death's door, Aldrovandi received from him
the seeds from a poppy plant that exuded a yellow liquid which
immediately blackened and looked like opium.[53]

The 1577 consignment also included specimens of various
minerals, plants, tree bark and shells. Some of these were credited
with medicinal properties, such as a cashew nut (believed to be an
aphrodisiac), a clay from Saxony that was used by surgeons to heal
broken bones, and a sulphur that was an antidote to the stings of
rays. An aromatic reed used in theriac gave Aldrovandi an opportunity for name-dropping: he had received it from Marcantonio
Barbaro, who was Venetian ambassador to the Ottoman Empire
and brother of the famous humanist Daniele Barbaro.[54] In return
for his 25 items, Aldrovandi asked Francesco for (parts of) plants or

their seeds, as well as a painting of the two snakes that he had been given by the Grand Duke because one of them had died before his own painter had been able to depict it; its dried remains had become an exhibit in his museum. Some idea of the practicalities involved can be gained from Francesco's reply in September 1578: Aldrovandi would have to wait because the Grand Duke's painter was involved in depicting plants, which had to be done in the summer months.[55] And wait he did; in February 1580 he was still asking Francesco for the painting of the two vipers.[56] Aldrovandi's further request for 'a porcelain vase of your invention' and a glass of mountain crystal points to Francesco's proud invention of the first soft-paste European porcelain in powder blue on a white ground; the presence of clay and kaolin among the items in Aldrovandi's collection is proof that he shared this particular interest with the Grand Duke.[57]

By the 1580s a widespread network was providing Florence and Bologna with plants and seeds. An interesting three-way exchange of objects was in place between Poland, Bologna and Florence with the dispatch of three paintings of an elk and two wild oxen from Poland and the skins of six Polish rodents and a weasel by a former student from Bologna, Martinus Fuxius, who was now working as a physician in Krakow.[58] In September 1583 Aldrovandi sent Francesco nineteen seeds that he had received from Spain and Flanders; two years later he was able to forward some seeds that he had received from Constantinople and from the Flemish botanist Charles de l'Écluse in Vienna. In 1586 he sent a further thirty seeds, some that he had received from a physician in Cairo, and other, Hungarian ones received from Clusius.[59] Although Aldrovandi and Clusius were not in regular contact, the latter was nevertheless particularly useful because of his own widespread network of correspondents and because his role in the service of the Habsburg court in Vienna, which was regularly engaged in diplomatic missions with the Ottoman sultan in Constantinople, brought him into direct contact with the rare bulbs from the Middle East that were beginning to enter Europe at this time.[60]

Besides these exchanges of *naturalia*, Aldrovandi repeatedly made requests to Francesco to use his influence in favour of his appointment as one of the Forty (*Quarantato*) of the Bolognese Senate, an honorific title that had a family history and that he hoped to secure for himself as well. In a similar vein, in December 1585 Aldrovandi wrote to Francesco asking him to support an increase in his university salary, 'bearing in mind the heavy burdens, expenses and studies of one who has already spent 33 years on courses on Aristotle and the philosophical history of plants, animals and minerals, which, God willing, I shall soon reveal to the world with a work on the marvels of the nature and art of the whole universe', which was nearing completion.[61]

Aldrovandi also hoped for financial patronage. In a letter to Bolognetti in 1576 he wrote:

> A patron would be required to have the woodcuts made of the images for insertion in the publications. I already have six thousand images, and they will amount to nine thousand if I manage to finish them all. They are incredible things for anyone who has not seen them. I have spent all my income on these valuable studies, and rest assured that I have spent more than ten thousand scudi in accumulating so many *naturalia*, and still spend more than three hundred scudi a year to this purpose.[62]

Francesco did indeed assist with the production of images by sending the Florentine artist Lorenzo Benini to Bologna to work for a couple of years on transferring images from Aldrovandi's collection of painted drawings to woodblocks for incision. In his last extant letter to Francesco de' Medici written in July 1587, three

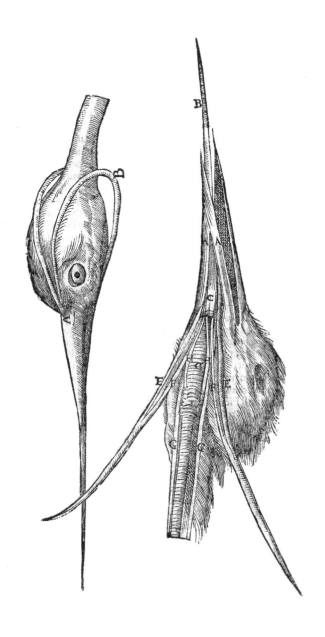

16 Woodpecker dissection, from Aldrovandi, *Ornithologiae hoc est de avibus historiae libri XII* (1599).

months before the suspicious deaths of the Grand Duke and his second wife, Bianca Cappello, on the same day, Aldrovandi sent him a sample print of three birds made from an incised woodblock on paper and silk.[63] In the letter, he went on to describe how he had dissected a woodpecker with a long retractable tongue to extract ants and other insects from inside the bark of trees, and could not resist adding that he had included an image of its anatomy in the book (illus. 16).[64]

In the introduction to his *Ornithology*, Aldrovandi gave due credit to Benini and others who had assisted with the production of the work, not failing to mention the great personal expense in which his activities involved him. And the first volume opened with a public expression of the author's gratitude to Francesco's successor, Grand Duke Ferdinando de' Medici, for having provided him with a live specimen of a golden eagle, the most noble of all birds, in early 1591. Its place as the first item in the book underscores not only Aldrovandi's indebtedness to his powerful patron but the naturalist's status as an authority on the natural world at the highest level. Nowhere is the interconnectedness of material exchanges and the question of patronage more evident than here.

Perfea seu Mamei Indorum
Quoyand colorado Hispanis.

FOUR

The American Mirage

America must have seemed far away from the land-locked area of Emilia-Romagna in which Bologna is situated. Perhaps the teenage Ulisse Aldrovandi dreamed of those far shores on the other side of the ocean when he arrived at Cape Finisterre on the west coast of Galicia. Closer to home, as we have seen, news about the New World and its unfamiliar objects caused a stir when they reached Bologna in the early 1530s. And in the following decade, the presence of Francisco López de Gómara as chaplain and librar-ian of the Spanish College of Bologna University enabled Aldrovandi to copy the Spaniard's manuscript on the conquest of America, 'Historijs Indicis', eight years before it went into print as *La historia de las Indias* in Zaragoza in 1552 (followed by an Italian translation in 1556).[1] He even attempted to obtain a dic-tionary of 'the language of the New World', blissfully ignorant of the number of different languages spoken in that continent.[2] Some idea of the excitement that the expeditions aroused can be gauged from the words of Juan Páez de Castro, a member of the retinue of the imperial envoy to the Council of Trent. After the return of Agustín de Zárate, author of a history of the European discovery of Peru, with 'very curious things and a great account of those parts', Páez de Castro wrote in October 1546: 'You will believe that I would like to see that world and that I do not give up hope of seeing it.'[3]

17 Sapote mamey, from Aldrovandi, *Tavole*, Biblioteca Universitaria Bologna.

Venice became a hub of publications on the New World early on. Girolamo Fracastoro's *Syphilis*, published there in 1530, was a poetic account of the voyage of Columbus that also went into the controversy on whether or not the disease was of American origin.[4] This would have been of particular interest to physicians and pharmacists like Aldrovandi and Calzolari because the antidote, guaiacum, was without doubt an American product. Antonio Pigafetta's account of the first circumnavigation of the globe and reports of the European expansion in America documented in the works of Gonzalo Fernández de Oviedo and Pietro Martire d'Anghiera were published in Italian in the 1530s; Giambattista Ramusio went on to include them in three volumes of his *Navigationi et viaggi*, all published in Venice in the 1550s and dedicated to Fracastoro.[5] In May 1556 Baccio Puccini wrote from what he described as 'out of the way Pistoia, where there is nothing noteworthy to be seen' to thank Aldrovandi for informing him about the publication of the first two volumes of the *Navigationi* and of the work of Guillaume Rondelet on fish.[6] Ramusio's work was considered of such vital importance for anyone who intended to write about *americana* that in April 1628 Johannes Faber wrote to Federico Cesi – both members of the Lincean academy that Cesi had founded in 1603 – asking him to send another of the Linceans to try to acquire the work before it was sold to other interested buyers.[7]

It was not just news of the exploits of Hernán Cortés and the other *conquistadores* that fired the imaginations of the Europeans, but also, and especially, reports of the riches of the new continent. Writing to Cardinal Paleotti in 1581, Aldrovandi referred to life-size statues and statuettes made in silver and gold of all the animals, plants and fish of the Inca realm.[8] Fourteen years earlier he had held up Alexander the Great as a model for Francesco de' Medici, but now it was the example of the idolatrous Inca that served as a stimulus to imitate nature. In the temple and garden

of Coricancha in Cuzco described by Pedro de Cieza de León and
other Spanish chroniclers, there were beautifully crafted gold and
silver corncobs that, untroubled by even the most violent winds,
symbolized the Inca control over nature.[9] So now, remarkably, a
New World ruler had replaced Alexander the Great as a model to
be followed: if a 'barbarian prince' desired representations of the
whole world of nature, Christian monarchs should follow suit in
commissioning representations of the whole of God's creation.

The Spanish Crown had already proposed setting up a commission to obtain information about what was known as New Spain
in the 1520s, resulting in 1532 in a description that is unfortunately
only known through later excerpts. A similar commission from the
following year included a request to provide visual representations
of 'everything that can be painted'.[10] But in spite of these and other
early attempts to document the Spanish territory abroad in all its
particulars, the expedition to New Spain led by the royal physician
Francisco Hernández between 1570 and 1577, which resulted
in descriptions of more than 3,000 species of plants alone, has
tended to overshadow these earlier endeavours. Mention of the
Spaniard's work in the second edition of José de Acosta's *Historia
natural y moral de las Indías* soon apprised the European scholarly
community of its existence. Acosta's text was rapidly translated
into a variety of languages (it was made known to English readers
in 1604), but when the by now elderly Aldrovandi was reading the
Italian translation that had just appeared in Venice in the summer
of 1596, he noted that the censors had omitted some items that
had featured in the original Spanish edition.[11] Some of the years
spent by Acosta in Peru had coincided with Hernández's stay in
Mexico, and there were parallels in their interest in the natural
resources of the respective Spanish territories, even if those of the
missionary Acosta extended beyond the predominantly medicinal
concerns of Hernández, who had been able to try out some of
the native medicines on his own person.

Apart from their intrinsic interest, such substances were of great importance to any of those who, like Aldrovandi and Calzolari, were preparing theriac, because they could offer alternatives to some of the ingredients that came from the Orient. For example, it might prove possible to use the plant known as Peruvian balsam to replace the wood and fruit of the opobalsam derived from an eastern tree, while American copal, a resin, might serve the same function to replace one of the oriental gums prescribed in the theriac recipe. Equivalences between different substances, or even between different types of the same substance, were difficult to substantiate, as can be illustrated by the example of Agustín Farfán. This Augustinian friar, who had studied medicine in the universities of Alcalá de Henares and Seville in Spain before setting out for New Spain in 1557, continued to practise medicine there until his death in 1604. He applied the medicine that he had learnt in the Iberian peninsula, but in writing a treatise on medicine especially for those inhabitants of Mexico who lived far from the reach of physicians and pharmacists, he resorted to the use of local medicines if others were not available.[12] Among these, as a cure for dysentery, he prescribed copal, but it is by no means certain that Farfán's copal was the same as that of Hernández. The profusion of different species from the New World left many a naturalist thoroughly bewildered.

Aware of the ambiguities and uncertainties contained in publications on New World plants and medicines, in 1567 Aldrovandi wrote to the Cardinal Protector of the Spanish College in Bologna applying for assistance in obtaining novelties from America not only through the Spanish court but from physicians and merchants who travelled between the two continents.[13] In the following year he recalled that Roberto Saliceti was supposed to be sending him some seeds from Madrid that he had received from the Viceroy of Mexico, and in the same year he hoped to receive an aloe from Scipione Sirvanti in Milan.[14] Aldrovandi

wrote to the Grand Duke of Tuscany in September 1577 that he
had received four images of Mexican trees from Portugal eight
years earlier, so they are further evidence of a surge in his interest
in the Americas around 1569 (illus. 17).[15]

When a dragon appeared in the Bologna area on the day of
investiture of Aldrovandi's relative Ugo Boncompagni as Pope
Gregory XIII, 13 May 1572, Aldrovandi promptly set down to
write a seven-book treatise on the dragon, which he dedicated
to Filippo Boncompagni, the cardinal nephew of the new pope.
This move was undoubtedly intended as a bid to obtain access
to the papal ear then and in the future.[16] Aldrovandi also tried to
get Giacomo Boncompagni, an illegitimate son of Gregory, to
appeal to his father in order to obtain support for the expedition
to the New World that the Bolognese naturalist had envisaged
some five years earlier, but that assistance was not forthcoming.[17]

By the end of the year Aldrovandi had received news of the
Hernández expedition and must have realized that all his hopes
of being sent to the Americas under the patronage of the pope
or the Spanish monarch were in vain. He had set his sights too
high; America was a mirage that receded continuously from view.
Even attempts to gain access to the material from the Hernández
expedition were largely unsuccessful. Only a few months before
the death of Aldrovandi's most important patron, Francesco de'
Medici, in 1587, Aldrovandi wrote to the Grand Duke of Tuscany
that Philip II of Spain had 'a book of paintings of various novel
plants, animals and other Indian things', with the suggestion that
Francesco might try to obtain copies of some of them through
the intervention of his ambassador in Spain. Aldrovandi's information came from the papal diplomat and Bishop of Piacenza,
Filippo Sega, who had seen the paintings during one of his missions to Spain in the early years of the decade. Francesco's reply
was brief: 'It would be difficult to be able to obtain copies of
plants and animals from that book of the King, and among the

other difficulties it would be difficult to find someone capable to do the job there.'[18] The words 'among other difficulties' are an understatement, for King Philip jealously guarded the paintings from the Hernández expedition.

When Aldrovandi heard that the successor to Hernández, Nardo Antonio Recchi, had brought an abbreviated and edited version of Hernández' text to Naples in 1589, he immediately wrote to Giovanni Battista della Porta in Naples for further news, but della Porta's evasive replies did little to enlighten him further.[19] According to the Neapolitan Lincean, Recchi had at first promised to give him a list of Peruvian simples, but then had second thoughts; he feared for his life in the light of Philip II's strict secrecy regarding the American materials. Instead, he attempted to fob Aldrovandi off with the image of a *remora* that had been caught by Neapolitan fishermen, who had great difficulty in detaching it from the fish to which it was stuck.[20] When Joachim Jungermann saw Recchi's images in 1591, the latter's reluctance to divulge them meant that Jungermann only managed to copy a few of them furtively.[21]

Aldrovandi did not give up and corresponded with others, such as Fabio Colonna in Naples, in the hope of gaining more information. A letter from Ferrante Imperato to Charles de l'Écluse in Leiden in January 1598 reveals that he had little success either; although he did manage to obtain a glimpse of around a hundred images of animals and plants in Recchi's possession, 'painted in very beautiful and lively colours, but crudely done', Recchi told him that he had no intention of publishing them.[22]

Aldrovandi's hopes of obtaining copies of the Hernández images were raised again in 1599 when Girolamo Mercuriale wrote to him:

> I am told that the highly gifted Daniel Froeschl will make a portrait of the other two little birds, if the Grand Duke, who has summoned him to Florence, does not send him

to Spain as he intends to copy a book of 1,200 figures of
exotic plants from the New World that they say is in royal
possession, and for which the dead king paid 60,000
scudi; and once His Highness has them, you will also see
them.[23]

By now Aldrovandi's hopes were in vain. The images in the Spanish
work did not see publication until their appearance in an abbreviated edition, illustrated with woodcuts and including a scientific
commentary on the plants by Colonna, in the well-known *Mexican
Treasury* first published by the Accademia dei Lincei in Rome in
1628. And when Tuscany became the first Italian state to send an
expedition to America under the command of Captain Robert
Thornton with a view to establishing a colony on the north-
eastern coast of South America in 1608, Aldrovandi had been
dead for three years, and the death of Ferdinando de' Medici in
1609 marked the end of Medici interest in an American colony.

AMERICANA IN EUROPEAN COLLECTIONS

Exotic items from the Americas began to flow into the Old World
from the 1520s on. Surviving inventories indicate that they were
dispatched in large numbers to the Habsburg nobility in their
courts in Spain, the Southern Netherlands and central Europe,[24]
while missionaries brought objects from New Spain to the papal
court in Italy. These might be objects remarkable for the use of
precious stones and metals, for the skill in their manufacture or
for the information they could convey about indigenous practices,
especially those relating to religion.

Some of them ended up in collections of curiosities, like the
cloaks made of animal skins, bows and arrows, maracas, or the
beak and plumage of a toucan that the French cosmographer
André Thevet brought back with him from Brazil in 1556.[25]

Information about new, unknown species of plants and animals was bound to intrigue anyone with an interest in natural history. Thus we find Calzolari begging Aldrovandi for an American opuntia cactus and an aloe for a friend in 1557.[26] Besides forming objects of curiosity when mounted in settings of precious metal, bezoar stones were much sought after for their alleged medicinal properties, and reports of bezoar stones from the stomachs of American camelids opened up the possibility of an alternative – perhaps less expensive – source to the oriental ones that arrived in the port of Venice. These and other bezoars featured in the collection of Calzolari in Verona, together with other *americana* such as the purgative *mechoacán*, the celebrated cure for syphilis guaiacum, 'rare and beautiful fans made from the leaves of American trees used by those queens of the Indies', and an item of headgear and a shirt both made of parrot feathers.[27]

The young Ferdinando de' Medici had already demonstrated at the age of seventeen that he shared the dynasty's predilection for *americana* when in 1567 he gave instructions to his agents in Spain to look for not only spices and aromatic essences for medicinal purposes, but ebony, ivory, bamboo, tortoise shell and pearls from which to carve figurines, as well as a featherwork painting. Six 'paintings from the Indies . . . painted with figures of animals and flowers of those countries' entered his collection in 1585.[28]

Tracing the entry and disposition of the various items in the house where Aldrovandi lived and kept his collection is difficult because the earliest comprehensive inventories date from after his death in 1605 and the transfer of the Aldrovandi collection from his home to the Palazzo Pubblico in Bologna. As far as *americana* are concerned, we can at least be certain about his toucan beak. Leone Tartaglini sent him the image of a 'pica del Berzil' around 1572, but Aldrovandi had a beak in three dimensions too.[29] In the *Ornithología*, one of the only two illustrated treatises published during his lifetime, Aldrovandi refers to the beak of a toucan 'in my museum' that he had received some years earlier as a gift from the promising young student Nicolaus Espiletus in Flanders (ORN, I, pp. 801–2). Like Mary, Queen of Scots, owner of a 'beik of a foule of India or Brasile',[30] André Thevet and Pierre Belon in France, Conrad Gessner in Switzerland, Teodoro Ghisi in Mantua and many other sixteenth-century collectors scattered over Europe, Aldrovandi had only the beak, not the whole bird. All the same, he included two woodcuts of the whole bird, one taken from Thevet's *Cosmographie universelle* and the other from Gessner's *Icones avium*. Gessner had received the beak from Giovanni Ferrerio, but how this Piedmontese tutor to the monks of Kinloss Abbey in Scotland came by it remains a mystery. At any rate, Gessner's artist grafted the beak on to a body that is, in fact, not a toucan's, and his fanciful composite of a non-existent bird was in turn used for the first of Aldrovandi's woodcuts (illus. 18).[31]

The use of feathered adornments was a regular feature of per-sonifications of America in representations of the four continents, as, for example, in Jacopo Ligozzi's preliminary drawing of Pope

18 Toucan, from Aldrovandi, *Ornithologiae hoc est de avibus historiae libri XII* (1599).

Boniface VIII receiving the Florentine ambassadors in 1295.[32]
The first of two Amerindians depicted in both the *Ornithologia*
and the *Monstrorum historia* is a male figure labelled in the woodcut
as a 'man of the woods' (*homo sylvestris*), a term regularly applied
to images of the wild men that peopled the European imagination (illus. 19). The coloured drawing on which it is based adds
more detail: 'Man of the woods from the New World wearing a
featherwork cap and setting out for war' (illus. 20). This time
the bright scarlet of the feathers is clearly visible, and once again
an inset explains the technique of their insertion in a mesh in
more detail. In both cases it is evidently the technical skill of
the artisans who crafted these items that attracts Aldrovandi's
attention. Indeed, his appreciation of the skill of the American
featherwork artists was so great that he considered them superior

19 Amerindian man, from Aldrovandi, *Ornithologiae* (1599).

to the legendary masterpieces of Apelles. While there was already a tradition of skilled working with feathers in many European courts and cities, the iridescence and brilliance of the plumage of American parrots, hummingbirds and quetzals introduced a new level of splendour to such products.[33]

Aldrovandi explicitly refers at this point to a headdress made of scarlet parrot feathers in the collection of Antonio Giganti. It makes an appearance in the image of a female Amerindian

20 Amerindian man, from Aldrovandi, *Tavole*, Biblioteca Universitaria Bologna.

(illus. 21), for which both the coloured drawing and the block of wood in which it was engraved are still extant, labelled 'Queen of the island of Florida'.[34] In the coloured drawing the chestnut colour of the mesh into which the scarlet feathers have been woven predominates, but the scarlet is still visible along the contour of the headdress (illus. 22). The inset of a section of the mesh with red feathers attached shows in more detail the structure of the artefact. Presumably, Aldrovandi's artist has faithfully copied Giganti's featherwork headdress, while the rendering of the bluish-green dress made of a kind of tree moss is stiff and schematic, and the woman's shoes are distinctly European. In other words, it is a composite image made up of the *ad vivum* representation of an artefact, inspiration deriving from several plates in the Florida

21 Amerindian woman, from Aldrovandi, *Ornithologiae* (1599).

R egna Insula Florida plumario
rita uelo.

section of the vast compilation *America* by the De Bry family (even
though the artefact probably came from Brazil), plus the artist's
own imagination.[35]

These two images appear here for their connection with birds,
and reappear in in Aldrovandi's *Monstrorum historia*. It is an example
of how Aldrovandi grouped his material as in a modern database;
if an item could be relevant to different categories, there was
nothing against repeating it in the respective volumes that dealt

22 Amerindian woman, from Aldrovandi, *Tavole*, Biblioteca Universitaria
Bologna.

with those categories. The two subsequent images of Amerindians in the *Monstrorum historia*, labelled 'Image of King Quoniambec' (illus. 23) and 'King among the Cannibals' (illus. 24), are both taken from Thevet's *Cosmographie universelle*, and were later reworked in more sophisticated engravings for the same author's collection of portraits of famous men.[36] For the author and editor of the *Monstrorum historia*, America had not ceased to be a continent peopled by monstrous beings.

Giganti and Aldrovandi moved in similar Bolognese circles after Giganti's entry in 1580 into the service of Cardinal Gabriele Paleotti, a close friend of Aldrovandi who gave him a now lost American featherwork image of St Jerome. Giganti may have given or sold certain of his American items to Aldrovandi. Other items will have been transferred to Aldrovandi's collection after the death of Giganti in 1598. They include the oldest American

23 King Quoniambec, from Aldrovandi, *Monstrorum historia cum Paralipomena accuratissima historiae omnium animalium* (1642).
24 'King among the Cannibals', from Aldrovandi, *Monstrorum historia*.

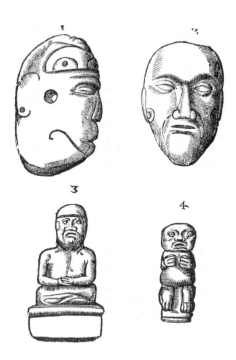

object in the Aldrovandi collection, one of a group of what are
described as 'stone idols of the New World in various shapes' in
the inventory of the Giganti collection. If an enthroned figurine
sitting on a quadrangular base (no. 3, illus. 25) is from the Olmec
culture, it must date from between 1200 and 400 BC and have
come from the region of Mexico later occupied by the Maya. This
would make the woodcut of this object in Aldrovandi's posthumous
publication on metals, *Musaeum metallicum*, the earliest image of an
Olmec artefact to be produced after the Spanish conquest.

   The 'idols' represented in the *Musaeum metallicum* were believed
to be lost until Davide Domenici discovered one of them while
browsing through the storerooms of the Museo Civico Medievale in Bologna at the beginning of 2020. It is a Mesoamerican

25 Four stone figurines, including one from Olmec culture (no. 3), from
Aldrovandi, *Musaeum metallicum in libros III distributum* (1648).

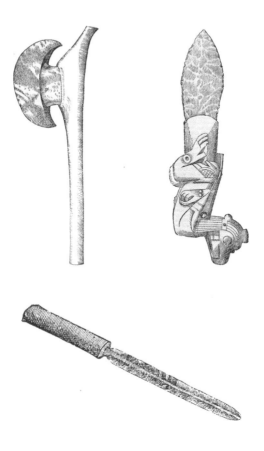

greenstone sculptural pendant in the form of a human head
that is a perfect match for the one (no. 1, illus. 25) depicted above
the enthroned figurine in the Aldrovandian woodcut and may
have come from the Mixtec culture of Mexico. At least eight,
and possibly all nine, 'idols' are of Mesoamerican origin.[37] Giganti
certainly gave Aldrovandi an Amazonian ceremonial stone axe
(transferred in 1878 to the former Museo Luigi Pigorini in Rome,
now the Museo della Civiltà), which Aldrovandi had admired

26 Amazonian axe, from Aldrovandi, *Musaeum metallicum*.
27 Mesoamerican stone knife with carved zoomorphic wooden handle,
from Aldrovandi, *Musaeum metallicum*.
28 Mesoamerican stone knife and handle, from Aldrovandi, *Musaeum metallicum*.

when he visited Giganti's studio in 1588; it was published with a woodcut labelled 'stone axe used in the sacrifices of the Indians' (illus. 26).

The pages of the *Musaeum metallicum* include a further three American items.[38] The first is a knife with a carved zoomorphic wooden handle (illus. 27), described in the 1586 inventory of Giganti's museum as 'a stone sacrificial knife with a wooden handle, one foot long'. Similar items in London and Rome have a socket for the insertion of the blade that is too weak to have permitted practical use as a sacrificial knife, so they may be assumed to have had a ceremonial function. The second knife (illus. 28) is longer and narrower and has a stone handle (Aldrovandi calls

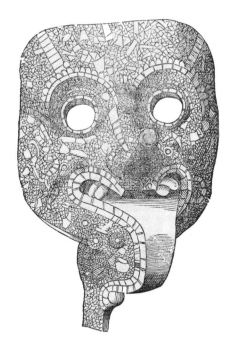

29 Long-nosed mask with mosaic decoration, from Aldrovandi, *Musaeum metallicum.*

it jade), corresponding to Giganti's 'stone razor'. Unfortunately, neither of these two knives is extant today, but the third item, a long-nosed mask with mosaic decoration (illus. 29), is now held in the Museo della Civiltà in Rome. It has been interpreted as a representation of the Nahua merchant god Yacatecuhtli because of the upturned, pointed nose and the extended, curved chin and given a likely place of origin in the Puebla-Tlaxcala Valley in Mexico.[39] Aldrovandi, however, was less interested in its iconography than in the technique of working with various little stones to create a mosaic. Like the featherwork headdresses and the knives, the mask too betrays a concern more for material and technique than for further ethnographic detail. All of this group of American artefacts go back to the arrival of a Spanish Dominican friar bearing gifts to Bologna in the early 1530s that was mentioned in Chapter One.

A study of the presence of American artefacts in early collections notes that 'of the thousands of American artefacts carried to Europe before the eighteenth century, fewer than 300 have survived to the present day.'[40] By comparison with the American items kept in roughly the same years by the French aristocrat Michel de Montaigne in his castle – hammocks, swords and sticks used in dancing – the number, quality and variety of Aldrovandi's *americana* is therefore exceptional, especially when we bear in mind that his was not a courtly collection.[41]

Besides artefacts, we have already seen how (parts of) American plants or images of them reached Aldrovandi through his correspondence network, with the first American specimens – tobacco, tomato, sweet pepper, maize, datura, agave, opuntia cactus, passion flower and others – arriving from the botanical gardens of Padua and Pisa at the beginning of the 1550s. In fact, thanks to the Aldrovandian material, it has proved possible to bring the date of the arrival in Italy of many American species forward by one or more decades.[42]

Later in the 1550s, Aldrovandi's friend the anatomist and herbalist Gabriele Falloppia (after whom the fallopian tube is named), who like Aldrovandi had been suspected of heresy as a young man, began asking Aldrovandi to favour his appointment to the chair of medicine in Bologna. A letter from Falloppia to Aldrovandi of October 1561 announced the arrival of a dozen cashews, some of which he promised to send him if Aldrovandi so wished. They had reached Falloppia by a circuitous route: the physician of 'Monsieur de Brissac' in Picardy had brought them to Picardy from Brazil, and from Picardy they had arrived in Padua, where Falloppia taught.[43]

Another friend of both Falloppia and Aldrovandi was the prefect of the Padua botanical garden, Melchiorre Guilandino. In February 1570 the consignment that he sent to Aldrovandi included not only various items that had been among the collector's list of desiderata, such as water parsley (*Oenanthe*) and a Peruvian sunflower, but some surprises: '*azulacho* from New Spain', tobacco from Brazil and the root of the *Ipomoea jalapa* (*mechoacán*, used as a purgative) 'which is so famous today' (BUB, MS 382, I, c. 149r). Three years earlier, Ippolito Salviani wrote that he had been the first in Rome to have the seed of an American plant that he called *Salviana*. He sent Aldrovandi two leaves of the plant, to which he attributed medicinal properties, as well as some of its seeds, with the promise to send some young plants if the seeds did not germinate in Bologna. It was a two-way exchange, as Salviani had successfully appealed to Aldrovandi for some seeds or young shoots of a blue clematis from Bologna, unaware that they were in the possession of Aldrovandi's arch-rival Cesare Odone.[44]

In 1586 Francesco de' Medici wrote to Aldrovandi about the misfortune of his guanábano tree:

Several years ago, while the Grand Duke Cosimo my lord and father was still alive, one of the fruits of the

guanábano was brought, and I took those seeds and had
them planted in a case. The plant sprouted and grew, with
leaves smaller than an orange tree but bigger than those
of a laurel, but because it was not tended with due care,
the plant perished.[45]

Francesco is referring to a period at least twelve years earlier,
as Cosimo died in 1574. This rendered him all the more grateful
for some guanábano seeds that Aldrovandi now sent him together
with a description of the tree. The guanábano is usually identified
with the soursop tree (*Annona muricata*) of the Americas, which
makes it all the stranger that Aldrovandi wrote that the tree
grew in Ethiopia. However, since he mentioned knives made
from 'Ethiopic stone' in his discussion of the two American
knives received from Giganti, while clearly referring to them as
Mexican ('in the Indian province of Themistitan'), he must be
using the term in a generic rather than a geographical sense (*MM*,
p. 157).

IMAGES OF *AMERICANA*

Besides the acquisition of American objects via Paleotti, Giganti
and others in Bologna, Aldrovandi drew on his many contacts
further afield to obtain images of American items as a substitute
for the real thing. Images of the macaws of Eleonora of Austria,
the wife of Duke Guglielmo Gonzaga, reached Aldrovandi in
1571 via the Mantuan lawyer Francesco Borsati, while images of
such American species as the pineapple, maize (*Zea mays*), avo-
cado and mango can be found among his collection of painted
drawings (illus. 30 and 31).[46]

 In 1580, while sending the Grand Duke an image of an elk,
Aldrovandi went on to explain that it was not the same as the
Brazilian tapir, 'an animal similar to a mule, with rather short

legs'.[47] Struggling to compare the New World tapir with Old
World counterparts, two French travellers to Brazil in the sixteenth
century, Jean de Léry and André Thevet, had likewise described
the tapir as half cow and half donkey.[48] Aldrovandi claimed that
the hoof of the elk was divided into two parts, while that of the
tapir was divided into three. The difference was crucial because
in the sixteenth century the nail of the elk was considered to be
the nail of the 'great beast' that could be ground into a powder
and used to treat epilepsy. It was precisely at this time that the
Milanese physician Apollonius Menabenus, who had had first-
hand experience of the elk in Sweden, published a treatise on the
anatomy and medicinal properties of the great beast, from which
Aldrovandi or his compiler quoted extensively in the chapter on
the elk in the posthumously published work on quadrupeds (*QBH*,
pp. 866–77).[49] Aldrovandi was naturally interested in the question
and hoped to obtain a painting of the animal *ad vivum* from Francesco
via the governors sent to the East Indies by the Portuguese king.

    Aldrovandi's images of American marine animals are par-
ticularly revealing of his treatment of his verbal and visual sources.
The image of a Brazilian marine monster in the *Monstrorum historia*
goes back to a coloured drawing in Aldrovandi's collection, labelled
'Human monstrous hermaphrodite with aquiline feet' (illus. 32/33).
It is clearly not a human, and is probably a South American sea
lion or fur seal.[50] That coloured drawing is derived from an Italian
or German illustrated broadsheet from the 1560s which was also
known to the Dutch marine expert Adriaen Coenen, who used
it in his *Whale Book* and his *Big Fish Book*.[51] The wounded creature,
as the Portuguese scholar Péro Magalhães de Gândavo recounted
on the basis of his years in Brazil, was attacked and killed by locals
when they saw it on the bank of a river in 1564. Both Coenen
and the German broadsheet show its attackers with a sword and
bows and arrows, but Aldrovandi's coloured image and the print
derived from it show only the creature in isolation on the page.

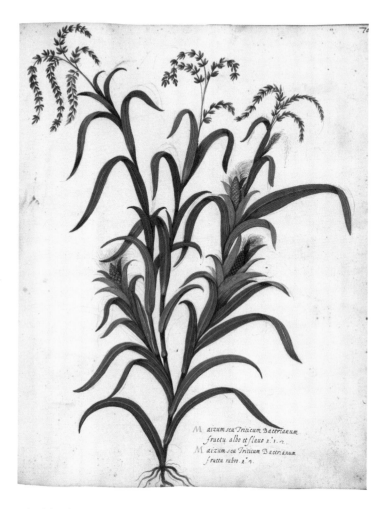

The bleeding wounds and two arrows sticking out of the creature's flank are the only remnants of the scene of the attack.

The Roman patrician Tommaso de' Cavalieri, in whose house Aldrovandi had seen some featherwork shields, sent him an image of a spiny American fish labelled 'Reversus indicus aculeatus'

30 Maize (*Zea mays*), from Aldrovandi, *Tavole*, Biblioteca Universitaria Bologna.

(illus. 34).[52] The collection of de' Cavalieri, who played an important part in the implementation of Michelangelo's redesign of the Campidoglio and owned a large number of the sculptor's draw-ings, was one of the collections of antiquities that Aldrovandi had visited during his early stay in Rome in 1550. The Bolognese

31 Pineapple, from Aldrovandi, *Tavole*, Biblioteca Universitaria Bologna.

naturalist recorded the Roman provenance on the painting and had it copied for his friend Giganti, and also sent a copy 'painted from life by my painter' to Francesco de' Medici in 1578.[53] Francesco reciprocated with a number of images, including two of American fauna and flora: the pineapple and the agouti ('Indian rabbit') by Ligozzi.

Aldrovandi accompanied his letter with a description of how the *reversus* was used to catch other fish in the sea in a similar way to the use of birds of prey in the air. So on this occasion he is writing less as a naturalist than as an ethnographer. Since the fish was easy to domesticate, the American natives tied a cord to its tail and projected it into the water so that it would hurl itself at other fish and spear them on its spikes. When they hauled in the rope, they could detach their catch and show their gratitude to the fish. Although Aldrovandi states that it attacks fish that are much larger than itself, the image shows an inordinately large

32 Brazilian sea monster of 1564, from Aldrovandi, *Monstrorum historia* (1642).

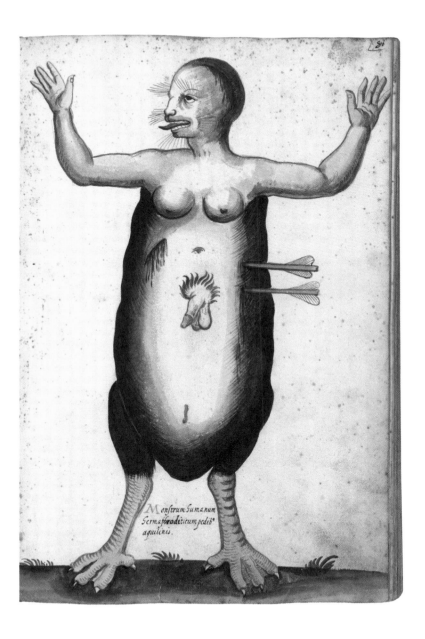

Monstrum humanum
Hermaphroditicum pedib.
aquilinis.

33 Brazilian sea monster, from Aldrovandi, *Tavole*, Biblioteca Universitaria Bologna.

spiky fish with what appear to be a number of smaller ones stuck to its spikes, although the presence of a seal among the captive prey suggests that the fish are meant to be large, which would make the spiny fish enormous. To confuse matters even more, Aldrovandi compares it with the spherical fish *orbis*, which was hung from the ceiling of many a *studiolo* because it was believed to work like a weathervane. Eight years later, in describing his visit to the collection of Giuseppe Casabona, he was still wondering whether the *orbis echinatus* might be related to the *reversus Indicus*.[54] Still, the lack of proportion and the naive style of the painting of the spiky *reversus* are not what count; it is designed to show a fishing technique, more like a diagram than a lifelike representation.

The same is true of a second image whose style suggests that it came from the same provenance (illus. 35). This *reversus Indicus* is a *remora*, an eel-like fish with a suction device that enables it to cling tenaciously to its prey, or even to the side of a ship. In 1577 Aldrovandi had apologized to the Grand Duke that he was unable

34 *Reversus Indicus aculeatus* ('spiky American remora'), from Aldrovandi, *Tavole*, Biblioteca Universitaria Bologna.

to send him a painting of a *remora* because his painter had been away and ill part of the time, but in the following year he was able to satisfy his request.[55] The painting shows two fishermen in a boat, one of whom has attached a cord to the neck of the *remora* to haul in the catch once the fish has captured its prey, in this case a seal, while a turtle watches from the water. The image is a faithful copy of a well-known woodcut that had appeared in a work by Conrad Gessner, and once again the disproportion is less important than the demonstration of a fishing technique like that using its spiny counterpart.[56] Although the *remora* was known to antiquity, Aldrovandi also records its Native American name, *guaiacano*, which is taken, like the rest of his account of the technique, almost word for word from one of the many works on America that formed part of his well-stocked library: the first book of *De orbe novo* by Pietro Martire d'Anghiera.[57] First published in 1511, the work must have circulated in manuscript form in Venice at an even earlier date, since the same account, with a marginal sketch of the fishing

35 *Reversus Indicus* ('American remora'), from Aldrovandi, *Tavole*, Biblioteca Universitaria Bologna.

technique, can be found in a manuscript by Alessandro Zorzi
from the very first years of the century reporting the discovery of
the New World.[58] Aldrovandi's account of the spiky *reversus* draws
on that other early chronicler of the Americas, Gonzalo Fernández
de Oviedo.

36 *Reversus Indicus squamosus* ('scaly American remora'), from Aldrovandi,
De piscibus libri v *et De cetis lib. unus* (1638).
37 *Reversus Indicus anguilliformis* ('eel-shaped American remora'),
from Aldrovandi, *De piscibus*.

When it came to illustrating these two types of American *remora* in his book on fishes (illus. 36 and 37), Aldrovandi's artist, no doubt acting on his master's instructions, removed the incongruities of size in the case of the spiny *reversus* by eliminating the seal stuck to one of its spikes. He also removed the fishing boats and the cord attached to the tail or neck respectively, thereby changing their function from illustration of a fishing technique to images of two varieties of fish. These changes reflect an intention to provide images that looked more scientific; in all other respects, however, the image of the *guaiacano* published in 1638 remained faithful to its by now antiquated source.

By definition, Aldrovandi's *americana* are exotic, and thus never at home. The artefacts, animals and plants, or parts of them, have been removed from their American setting. In the case of the printed images of the *remora*, they have been removed from a painted setting that illustrates an example of a fishing technique. Their appearance as isolated images on an otherwise blank page is familiar to us from the format of modern scientific illustration. However, as Florike Egmond has argued, it would be wrong to see the decontextualized image as necessarily secondary to a prior composite one.[59] In the case of Aldrovandi's *remora*, the coloured image embedded in a context, that of fishing, was subsequently detached (by his editor) to function as a type image in a black-and-white work on the different types of fish. However, in the last decades of the sixteenth century, the British artist John White, who had been in America, reversed the direction by using his isolated and detailed studies of different fishes in a composite scene representing different fishing techniques.[60] The process of decontextualization or recontextualization was thus a two-way one.

Et se nul se vaulst nō tīrreeson de ... ... ce q̄ ceū reūt nō est hitablis.

aie len ne co ita[v]
re en quelque ma
mere quī teng̃tet
dee antwodes.

FIVE

Anomalies

riting to Grand Duke Francesco de' Medici in 1585, Ulisse Aldrovandi reported that besides two gazelles, a male and a female, with a six-day-old fawn, he had also seen in Bologna an 'Indian pig with an aperture on top of its back instead of in its natural place with which it urinates, but I believe that it is a monster'. He duly had them all depicted by his painter 'because they greatly pleased me, nor had I ever seen animals like them'. And during his second stay in Florence the following year, he laconically commented that in the courtyard of the Medici palace he had seen 'a monstrous boy from Poland'; during the same visit he saw in the collection of Gori Bamberini 'a monstrous euphorbia'.[1]

The 'Indian pig' is the South American peccary, which is depicted in one of Aldrovandi's coloured drawings emitting a jet of what he supposed was urine from its back.[2] Unfamiliar with the peccary's dorsal scent gland, he applied the epithet 'monstrous' to what we now know is a natural feature. By the time that the image was used for a woodcut in the *Monstrorum historia*, the orifice in its back has become a rudimentary navel that emits an unspecified 'watery liquid' (illus. 39).[3] In the case of the Polish boy, 'monstrous' must refer to some physical deformity. And the 'monstrous euphorbia' was presumably anomalous in some other way, like one of the thirty 'monstrous' plants or fruits illustrated in the *Monstrorum historia*. In short, the term 'monstrous'

38 Augustine preaching to the Antipodes, illumination from a French translation of *De civitate Dei*, 15th century.

could cover a wide range of phenomena in the human, animal and plant worlds.

In his comprehensive natural history, Pliny the Elder had devoted Book 7 to the human animal, as distinct from other animals, with an emphasis on the exceptional, such as giants and dwarves.[4] In the previous book he had compiled a long list of various peoples of the world whose bodies were characterized by some extraordinary feature: a single foot or eye, having the head of a dog or a pig, with their faces on their chests, and so on.[5]

The popularity of Book 7 in the sixteenth century is already attested by the publication of a separate edition of it in Krakow in 1526, followed soon afterwards by editions in the vernacular. Despite the status of Pliny as an ancient authority, however, he was not a Christian, so the debate among theologians such as St Augustine followed a different course. They were concerned with such questions as whether deformity was the result of sin, or whether there could be people (Antipodes) living upside down,

39 Collared peccary, from Bartolomeo Ambrosini, *Paralipomena*, appendix to Aldrovandi, *Monstrorum historia* (1642).

as it were, on the lower surface of the globe (illus. 38).[6] With the European discovery of America, similar questions arose of whether its inhabitants were descended from Adam, and from Columbus onwards the physical appearance of some of the ethnic groups in South America was assimilated to that of some of the Plinian races. By the end of the century, at least four of them had become consolidated as representative of the American continent: headless people, female warriors (Amazons), cannibals and (Patagonian) giants.[7]

Aldrovandi's position on the monstrous races is difficult to determine because assertions made in the *Monstrorum historia* may be due to the editor of that posthumous work, Bartolomeo Ambrosini, rather than to Aldrovandi himself. Given the limited range of his travels, he was hardly in a position to confirm or deny the existence of monstrous races on his own authority. So when André Thevet, who had spent a brief ten weeks in the New World, reported that he had never seen the single-eyed Cyclopes there, but St Augustine accepted their existence, all Aldrovandi/ Ambrosini could do was record the differing views (*MH*, p. 12). In other cases the work betrays attempts to naturalize them: the mouthless people must have had very small mouths that became exaggerated in the travellers' tales; the resemblance of monkeys to humans afforded a means to explain away some of the shaggier Plinian races; and so on.[8] Still, if one could not be certain whether or not a people existed, it was at least possible to include an image and leave the rest to the reader.

Images of Plinian monstrous races or individual monsters had featured sporadically in the visual record long before Aldrovandi's time, but the sixteenth century saw the appearance of several publications in which woodcuts represented their variety, from the chronicle of Sebastian Franck and the cosmography of Sebastian Münster to the catalogue of prodigious events by Conrad Wolffhart in the middle of the century. Closer to Aldrovandi,

both thematically and chronologically, was Ambroise Paré, a surgeon in the French royal court and author of a work on monsters
and marvels that was first published in 1573. It ran into many
editions and was thus able to include some of the woodcuts and
information about the strange-looking fauna of the New World
from the works of André Thevet, who served in the same court.[9]
Aldrovandi's editor recycled several of these by now outdated
images to represent individual monsters of his own day in an
appendix to the *Monstrorum historia*. He extended Aldrovandi's
catalogue to include further birds and insects, marine and terrestrial
animals, drawing largely on woodcuts in Paré's work that were in
turn derived from André Thevet's *Cosmographie universelle*, as well
as adding more recent information such as a Jesuit report on a
monstrous serpent seen near Tunapuna in Trinidad in 1628.[10]

Monstrorum historia opens with woodcuts of a number of the
Plinian races: people without a mouth who live off the scent of
fruit and flowers; people with tiny mouths who have to take their
sustenance through a straw; people with an elongated lower lip,
extended ears, four eyes or one eye, the neck of a crane or reversed
feet. Although these are human groups, the same images were
used to illustrate examples of individual monstrous births, a topic
in which Aldrovandi as a physician was very interested: those born
with two heads, Siamese twins or those whose feet were turned
backwards instead of forwards. There was no clear dividing line
between the two categories: both individuals and groups could
be characterized by the same abnormality.[11]

Among the 'rules of composition' of these anomalous humans
or animals was multiplication or subtraction: for example, a human
or animal might possess more body parts than the usual number,
such as a two-headed calf, or fall below the norm. In the first
volume of his *Ornithologia*, Aldrovandi used one of the two coloured
drawings in his collection of the head of a rhinoceros hornbill
(illus. 40). He placed it after his discussion of the American

40 Rhinoceros hornbill, from Aldrovandi, *Tavole*, Biblioteca Universitaria Bologna.

toucan, noted above all for its long beak. The hornbill, which is found in Africa and Asia but not in America, not only has a long bill, but the horny casque from which it gets its name suggests an incipient second bill on top of the first. Whatever Aldrovandi made of this, the bird was certainly unlike any other he had seen. He claimed to have received the two drawings from persons who had witnessed the Battle of Lepanto in 1571 (ORN, I, p. 804).[12]

The five images of different types of bird of paradise, on the other hand, that immediately follow Aldrovandi's discussion of the hornbill all show the bird without any feet (ORN, I, pp. 810–15). The earliest European accounts of the bird of paradise, the 'bird of God' (manucodiata), which is endemic to New Guinea and the Moluccan archipelago, stem from the Suma Oriental of Tomé Pires, written between 1512 and 1515, and a visit to the Moluccas by Ferdinand Magellan in 1522 during the first circumnavigation of the globe. Remarkably, the bird made its appearance in a European collection within a year or two, as it is recorded in the 1523–4 inventory of the possessions of Margaret of Austria in Malines.[13] None of these early accounts mentions a lack of feet, but Maximilian Transylvanus, a secretary to Emperor Charles V, reported that they were in perpetual flight. This, and the fact that preserved specimens of the bird were not always complete, probably gave rise to the belief in the footless bird of paradise that was perpetuated, with variations, by Pierre Belon, Conrad Gessner (whose woodcut of the bird of paradise is one of the five Aldrovandian printed images, illus. 41), Ambroise Paré (who had one in his collection) and others. It was not until various complete dried specimens began to arrive in the port of Amsterdam that Carolus Clusius was able to correct the belief, which he had himself entertained until then, that they did not have feet, although neither of the only two images of them that he published in his Exoticorum libri decem (1605) has feet.[14] The image of the miraculous bird emigrated from the scientific literature to books of emblems and

artistic decoration, featuring, for example, in the grotesque frescoes by Prospero Fontana in the Palazzo di Firenze in Rome, or those attributed to Antonio Tempesta in the eastern corridor of the Galleria degli Uffizi in Florence.[15]

An example of excess rather than lack that spans both anomalous human groups and individuals is that of people with an unusual amount of body hair. The eighth-century *Liber monstrorum*, a compendium of prodigies, includes a brief section titled 'On bearded women': 'Near a mountain in Armenia, women are (said to be) born who are covered in hair and with a beard hanging down to their breasts.'[16] In the eleventh century the German chronicler Adam of Bremen situated bearded women in the mountains of

41 Fifth type of (footless) bird of paradise, from Aldrovandi, *Ornithologiae hoc est de avibus historiae libri XII* (1599).

Norway, while two centuries later the Dominican friar Thomas
of Cantimpré placed them in the forests of India.[17] And, on the
eve of the sixteenth century, in his *Liber chronicarum* the humanist
and physician Hartmann Schedel cited the authority of Pliny,
Augustine and Isidore of Seville to include a woodcut of 'a woman
with a long beard that hangs down to her breast'.[18] On the other
hand, Pliny and other Roman authors record cases of women
who at some point in their lives developed male characteristics,
including a beard.

Perhaps the best-known of these cases is one recorded by both
Ambroise Paré and his near contemporary Michel de Montaigne
of a young Frenchman called Germain Garnier, who sported a
dense red beard. His parents had brought him up in the small
village of Vitry-le-François in Champagne as a girl called Marie.
When Marie was fifteen years old, she jumped too vigorously over
a ditch, leading to the extrusion of a penis that had remained
concealed inside her until then.[19] When Montaigne returned
to the village in 1580, he was not able to see Garnier, but he
recorded that the local girls used to sing a song warning of the
dangers of taking long strides.[20] The interest shown in the case
of Marie/Germain indicates the extent to which the scientific
writers with their cabinets of curiosities and the broadsheets and
popular songs of the time shared a fascination with what were
regarded as monstrous forms of humanity – an instance of the
convergence between popular and learned culture.

The existence of individuals with some kind of physical
deformity was solidly attested closer to home; these people were
bound to interest Aldrovandi because of his study of medicine
and the dissections that he carried out on dead animals. The
interest in making portraits of them is attested by Francisco
Hernández, who practised medicine in Toledo before being
dispatched to New Spain in 1570. On a nine-year-old bearded
girl he had seen in Toledo and who died soon afterwards, he

commented: 'many saw her because they portrayed her naked.'[21] Among the numerous coloured drawings that Aldrovandi collected during his lifetime are three of women with hairy faces. The first woman, like in the cases discussed by Pliny and other Roman authors, was not born hairy but developed a beard at the age of nine. Aldrovandi's painted version of her shows a woman of about twenty years old who sports a dense beard and moustache, while her temples show a receding hairline. The drawing was sent to him by the physician Gisbert Voss von Vossenburg, who gives the woman's name as Helena, in 1598, and was probably a gift from Maria Anna of Wittelsbach to William V, Duke of Bavaria, as a token of gratitude for his having sent her a series of portraits of a family of hairy people in 1583.[22]

More can be said about the case of several anomalous births within a single family (to which Helena was not related).[23] Among a group of nine portrait paintings recorded in the inventory of the library of Ferdinando, Palazzo Ducale, Mantua, compiled in 1626–7, is one described as being of 'a hairy woman' from the collection of Vincenzo I Gonzaga. It shows a young girl, her face covered with fine hair, holding a sheet of paper with a text written in the first person to introduce herself. She gives her name as Anton(i)etta, and states that she is in the service of a grand lady, no less than Isabella Pallavicino, Marchesa di Soragna, who resided in Parma from 1593. Among the travels of the marchesa, on which she was accompanied by the girl, was a visit to stay with the senator Mario Casali in Bologna in April 1594. On that occasion they called on Aldrovandi. He was able to carry out an examination of the physical appearance of the young girl, who must have been about six years old at the time.

Antonietta was a daughter of Pedro González, a native of Tenerife, who claimed the title 'Don' because of his descent from the local ruling elite before the arrival of the Spaniards. The Nuremberg physician Hieronymus Münzer gives us a vivid picture of Valencia's trade in slaves from the Canaries in 1494,[24] and it may be supposed that Pedro's parents underwent a similar fate. Though his parents were smooth skinned, Pedro was born suffering from congenital *hypertrichosis universalis*, a condition that persisted in some, but not all, of his children, and even down to the third generation in the case of a grandchild christened Giacomo.

While still a boy, Pedro González was given by the Spanish king to Henri II of France in 1547, and the family was passed on to his successor and subsequently to Catherine de' Medici. After her death the family was sent to Parma. Reluctant to remain at court as a curiosity, Pedro asked for employment, and was given the job of superintendent of the Farnese farm in Collecchio. When his son Enrico was given a similar post in Capodimonte on Lake Trasimeno, Pedro spent his last days there after joining him with the rest of the family.

As a physician, Aldrovandi, who had a piece of the hairy human skin of a 'man of the woods' in his collection, was bound to take a lively interest in such a family (*MH*, p. 16). They provided him with valuable information about the genetic transmission of excessive facial hair, on which he drew for his *Monstrorum historia*, where he notes: 'That happened recently in Parma in the Farnese court, where a girl with a hairy face . . . gave birth to some babies with completely hairy faces.' (*MH*, p. 473).

Four of them are illustrated in woodcuts in that work. We find Antonietta depicted in full length in a woodcut, where she is credited with an age of eight years (illus. 42). The woodcut matches one of the coloured drawings, where the text runs: 'Twenty-year-old woman with a hairy face like a monkey but smooth on the rest of her body' (illus. 43). In spite of the discrepancy in age (it should be remembered that the *Monstrorum historia* was compiled long after Aldrovandi's death by Ambrosini), the embroidered dress and the flowers in the girl's hair make it clear that they are both representations of the same person.

A second woodcut in the *Monstrorum historia* of a 'hairy girl' credits her with an age of twelve years. This woodcut is less elaborate than the previous one. Zapperi identifies the girl as Francesca. Her elder brother Enrico is depicted beside his father, Pedro, in the first woodcut of this series (illus. 44). The Swiss physician Felix Platter had the opportunity to examine Francesca, Enrico and their mother when they were on their way to Parma in 1591.

42 Antonietta González, who suffered from congenital *hypertrichosis universalis*, from Aldrovandi, *Monstrorum historia* (1642).

M ulier uiginti annorum
capite Simiam imitante
corpore glabro.

43 Antonietta, from Aldrovandi, *Tavole*, Biblioteca Universitaria Bologna.

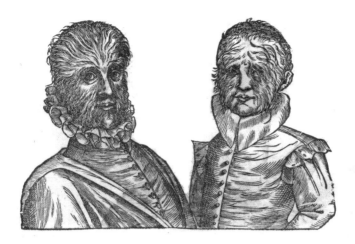

The presence of these three consecutive woodcuts at this point jars with the surrounding material. After the insertion of the González family, he continues with a hairy man and woman whom he calls Cinnamini. Whether the order is due to Aldrovandi or to Ambrosini, the individual members of the González family are out of place here, sandwiched as they are between several human groups Moreover, their scientific value is close to zero: the only information that a reader could derive from them is that some people have excessive facial hair, just as others have an excessive number of eyes, and that it appears to be congenital. It is only hundreds of pages later that the author returns to the question of congenital hairiness.

DRAGONS, BASILISKS, UNICORNS

While the available information and images of the González family are convincing enough, there are a number of items in Aldrovandi's and other collections that are closer to myth than reality. In the case of the ubiquitous and much coveted horn of

44 Pedro and Enrico González, who were born with the congenital condition *hypertrichosis universalis*, from Aldrovandi, *Monstrorum historia* (1642).

the unicorn, Aldrovandi mentions those in the collections of the king of Poland, the Venetian Republic and the Duke of Mantua, but argues that it is from the marine unicorn, a term referring to the narwhal.[25] Thus he was aware that the 'horns of unicorns' in the various collections were the tusks of a particular type of whale. This example, taken from a letter of Aldrovandi to Girolamo Mercuriale in 1599, indicates his eagerness to subject received opinion to scientific scrutiny, in marked contrast to the image of a credulous Aldrovandi that emerges from the mass of images in the posthumous works that were inserted by his later editors and could be a century or more old. It should be noted, for example, that although Ambrosini records and includes the image of a one-eyed marine dragon sent to Aldrovandi by Bishop Cesare Bovio, Aldrovandi did not include it in his work on marine animals (illus. 45).

One of the most popular items to be singled out for comment by visitors in the seventeenth century was the dragon that had made an appearance near Bologna on the day in 1572 that coincided with the investiture of Pope Gregory XIII and had been entrusted to Aldrovandi to display in his museum.[26] He had it painted (illus. 46), and was not slow to send copies to such distinguished figures as Duke Alfonso II of Ferrara as a way of elevating his own status, though his projected publication on the dragon did not see the light of day until 1639. For Aldrovandi, what was monstrous was the presence of two feet on a creature

45 Marine dragon, from Bartolomeo Ambrosini, *Paralipomena*, appendix to Aldrovandi, *Monstrorum historia* (1642).

that was classified as a serpent, but he went on to interpret this unusual feature as a sign of the creative power of nature. Therefore, we cannot take 'monstrous' to mean 'unnatural', if nature itself is capable of producing it. 'Out of the ordinary' comes closer to its range of meanings.

While the Bolognese dragon was, at least for Aldrovandi, a natural phenomenon, he was in no doubt about the artificial nature of another monster, as the caption in the painted drawing of it clearly states: 'dried ray in the form of a dragon fabricated by charlatans' (illus. 47). Aldrovandi also had no doubt about the origins of a monster reputed to have been found in the River Tiber in Rome in 1496. This composite creature – made up of the head of a donkey, one human hand and one animal limb, one cow's hoof and one clawed foot, one woman's breast and belly, fishy scales on its arms and legs, and a dragon-like tail with a grotesque head with horns and a beak emerging from its rear – defies all belief (illus. 48). Aby Warburg was the first to notice a

46 Bolognese dragon seen near Bologna in 1572, from Aldrovandi, *Tavole*, Biblioteca Universitaria Bologna.

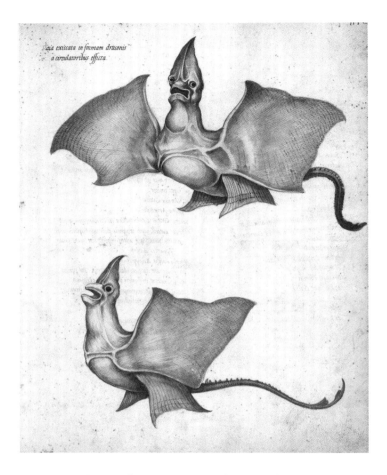

century ago that the figure was derived from an effigy of a Byzantine emperor in the twelfth-century Leonine Oracles.[27] In the *Monstrorum historia*, Ambrosini connected its concoction with the pamphlet war between Catholics and Protestants. In 1523 Philip Melanchthon published it together with a calf misbirth that had been variously interpreted as a pro-Lutheran or anti-Lutheran portent by the opposing factions. For Melanchthon, who set the monster against

47 Dragon fabricated from a dried ray, from Aldrovandi, *Tavole*, Biblioteca Universitaria Bologna.

the background of Castel Sant'Angelo and the Tiber flowing
below it, the ass's head stood for the pope, the naked female belly
stood for the dissolute lives of the whole papal hierarchy from
the head to priests and monks, and so on.[28] The authors of the
Monstrorum historia, on the other hand, could interpret the monster
as a symbol of the danger to the true faith posed by the new dis-
sident movement: 'The ass's head of this monster signified frigidity
and sloth, of which Luther and his followers had plenty; for with
all charity frozen . . . they brought destruction to Germany and
to many kingdoms.' (*MH*, p. 367).

Another monstrous figure with a long history was the seven-
headed hydra. Aldrovandi illustrated two of these on facing
pages of his *Serpentum et draconum historiae* to facilitate comparison.
He clearly indicates what he thought about the authenticity of

48 Monster found in the Tiber in 1496, from Aldrovandi, *Monstrorum
historia* (1642).

the first with the heading 'Seven headed hydra from Gessner very skilfully made and kept in the Venetian treasury'. He added that, although he thought it worthwhile to include the descriptions and images of several hydrae in his work, he considered them all to be artifices (illus. 49). The source of the image printed by Gessner in 1553 was a broadsheet stating that the hydra had been sent from Turkey to Venice and subsequently offered to François I of France in 1530. The story and the image were repeated by Conrad Wolffhart and others before reaching Aldrovandi, though curiously none of these writers claimed to have seen the actual object. Aldrovandi's statement that it had been bought back by the Venetians is taken from a later (1587) edition of Gessner, though the Swiss naturalist repeated that he had not seen it for himself and did not know whether the details provided by his informant were true or not. In fact, the only person who claimed to have seen it in person is Pierre Dan in a catalogue of what remained of the contents of the cabinet of curiosities of the castle of Fontainebleau in 1642. He contradicted the assertion that it had been repurchased by the Venetians, for

49 Seven-headed hydra, from Aldrovandi, *Serpentum et draconum historiae* (1640).

he – the only eyewitness among all these authorities – had seen the dismal remains of the royal hydra, minus its seven heads after the devouring activity of rats, with his own eyes in Fontainebleau.[29]

Gessner's broadsheet source warned that a fortune teller would be able to deduce that the appearance of the hydra was a warning of trouble with the Turks. In 1530, however, a more topical subject was the recent outbreak of the Reformation. It is therefore hardly surprising that the image was repeatedly used by Luther and his followers to equate the pope with the seven-headed beast on which the whore of Babylon rides in the *Apocalypse*.[30] When the revolt against Spanish rule broke out in the northern Netherlands in the 1560s, one of the slogans of the rebels was 'Sooner Turks than Papists', which shows that the hydra could be deployed in various polemical contexts to designate the enemy.

As late as 1617, an anonymous pamphlet published in London interpreted the beaching of a sperm whale near the port of Harwich as a warning against those who 'live in Atheisme, Papisme, and Epicurisme' whose 'outragious enormities dayly provoking our most iust GOD to power forth the consuming Vials of his incensed heauie indignation vpon all the misgouerned Sonnes of sinnefull Men'. The author concludes: 'Now whether this Monster of the Sea bee ominous or not, J had rather leaue to the wise and learned then my selfe determine.'[31] Like the figure of Marie/Germain discussed by Montaigne, such examples straddled the divide between popular and learned culture.

Although most of the *Monstrorum historia* is taken up with terrestrial and marine anomalies, strange and portentous celestial phenomena are not absent either. A chapter on 'celestial monsters', which was not included in the earlier editions of Ambroise Paré's *Des Monstres et prodiges*, made its first appearance in that of 1579, in which the French surgeon mentions the 'disfiguration of the face of the sky by bearded or hairy comets, flaming torches, columns, lances, shields, battles in the clouds, dragons, double moons and

suns and other things that I have not wanted to omit in order to complete this book of monsters'.[32] The accompanying woodcut, as he acknowledges, goes back to Conrad Wolffhart's collection of portents from mid-century. We find a very similar 'portentous and horrible comet' in the *Monstrorum historia* (illus. 50). The accompanying text speculates that they may be due to sunspots 'which many have observed with an excellent telescope'. As is well known, the telescope made its first appearance in the Italian

50 Portentous comet, from Aldrovandi, *Monstrorum historia* (1642).

peninsula in Venice in the second half of 1609, and Giovanni
Battista della Porta was able to show Federico Cesi one of his
own making in Naples in the following year. The term 'telescope'
itself does not seem to have been coined before 1611, the year in
which Galileo Galilei demonstrated the use of his telescope on
the Janiculum Hill in Rome.[33] Given that Aldrovandi was dead
before then, this whole passage must be the work of Ambrosini.

THE IMAGE NOT MADE BY HUMAN HAND

Another area of anomalies or wonders that demonstrated the
creative power of nature was the image made by chance, as it has
been called, or the image not made by human hand. Like the
Plinian races, this notion had a long ancestry. Pliny recounted the
story of the Greek artist Protogenes, the rival of Apelles. When
baffled by the difficulty of how to represent the foam emerging
from the jaws of an enraged dog, he threw a sponge at the painting,
an action which, by chance, produced exactly the desired effect.
Lucretius and Philostratos of Athens wrote about the way that
clouds could assume the shapes of fearsome giants, towering
mountains and other wonders. In the fifteenth century Leon
Battista Alberti explained the origin of sculpture in the perception
of tree trunks, clods of earth and similar objects that suggested
recognizable shapes and could, with only slight intervention, be
made to actually represent those objects.[34] The eccentric Piero di
Cosimo too is credited by Vasari with having been fascinated by
the shapes produced on walls by the spittle of sick people or in the
clouds and to have derived the forms of fantastic cities and other
subjects from them.[35] And in the sixteenth century the equally
eccentric ceramicist Bernard Palissy drew on his background in
painting on glass for his knowledge of the effect of heat on various
minerals. He put it to good use in allowing the coloured enamels
applied to the inner walls of one of the grottos in the garden

design described in his *Recepte véritable* to melt under the influence
of a central fire and to form random patterns. Palissy had a collection of minerals – unusually, the only systematic component of his
collection, in contrast to the heterogeneity of the cabinets of curiosities of his time – and compiled a rational catalogue of them.
This is one of the earliest systematic catalogues of a collection,
pre-dating Samuel Quiccheberg's of 1565 by two years.[36]

While the images produced in the clouds were entirely the
work of nature, a limited role could be left for the human hand
to bring to perfection the rudimentary images inscribed in trees,
rocks, flowers, plants and other materials. At a time when the possibility of a truce between Spain and the Netherlands after seventy
years of hostilities was in the air, Peter Paul Rubens remarked
that some unusual natural phenomena were being interpreted
by the people as a sign of the need to turn back to obedience to
the Catholic faith. One of these was the shapes observed in a
section of a sawn tree, 'which bear some resemblance to nuns
and monks with two violins'.[37]

It is not surprising that Aldrovandi also took an interest in
these images not made by human hand. He devoted several pages
of the *Musaeum metallicum* to pieces of marble containing zoomorphic or anthropomorphic images, such as the image from the
church of St John in Pisa of 'a hermit with another human effigy
in marble' which 'appears to have been delineated from life by
nature' (illus. 51). We can be certain that this image is not a later
insertion by Bartolomeo Ambrosini since it can be found among
the painted drawings in Aldrovandi's collection.[38] These images
were not confined to the religious sphere: another painted drawing
in Aldrovandi's collection is of a stone that he called *cynites* because
of the appearance of what looks like the front part of a dog on it;
this too appears in the *Musaeum metallicum* (illus. 52).[39] Not surprisingly, Athanasius Kircher included slightly modified versions
of the hermit and other religious figures in his *De lapidibus* of 1665,

51 Human figures in marble, from Aldrovandi, *Musaeum metallicum in libros III distributum* (1648).

less than twenty years after the publication of Aldrovandi's *Musaeum metallicum*, and in the eighteenth century the Spanish court painter Antonio Palomino collected a large number of examples like these in his *Museo pictórico* of 1715.[40]

Not only stones but living creatures could be inscribed by nature in a similar way. Among the painted drawings in Aldrovandi's collection is one of a tuna with images of various ships 'inscribed by nature' on its side (illus. 53). It is based on an illustrated pamphlet published in 1565 by Matthäus Franck in Augsburg. Aldrovandi is evidently drawing on this woodcut for the dimensions and other information about the wondrous find. The same image can be found in the *Whale Book* of Adriaen Coenen from 1585, in which Coenen's rendering of the German text of the pamphlet runs:

I, Johan Frutuoso, royal notary, a resident of this noble city of Gibraltar, attest and witness to all who shall see this that it is the truth. Certain information has been given to me, the notary of the court of law of this city, by six witnesses clearly indicating that 15 or 16 days ago a tuna was found on the coast of the sea in the city of Ceuta on which are painted, as it were, many galleys, masts, oars, rowers, artillery and more vessels and an armed galliot which appeared to want to storm one another. This was all done

52 Dog shapes in *cynites* stone, from Aldrovandi, *Musaeum metallicum* (1648).

in a natural and realistic manner as if a drawing had been made on the skin and flesh of this tuna in a wondrous way, never seen before. Done in Gibraltar, 13 May 1565, and below I have set my signature as a witness to its truth, signed Johan Frutuoso.[41]

If ships could be inscribed by nature on a fish, fish could be inscribed on other things in the same way. Bound in the same volume of coloured drawings as the tuna is a stone slab 'containing the impression of a *Passer* fish delineated by nature'.[42] Pierre Belon had already described and illustrated the Passer, noting that the Romans of his day still called it a Passera,[43] from the resemblance of its brownish colour to that of the sparrow (also called *Passer* in Latin). What Aldrovandi is describing has been identified as a member of the extinct *Vomeropsis* genus of prehistoric bony fish from the Eocene era; in other words, it is what we would today call a fossil (*MM*, p. 453).

A second fossil fish appears at the centre of a page with shells, rocks and other objects from various places (illus. 54). Coloured in dull yellow and grey against the blue-grey background of a piece of stone, it is taken from a work on fossils that Conrad Gessner planned to write, but when he died from the plague in Zurich in 1565 only the preliminary essay had been completed, although the inclusion of some two hundred images made it the most richly illustrated geological work of the sixteenth century.[44] The fossil stone in Gessner's work is called *Lapis Islebianus*, an indication that it had been found in Eisleben in Saxony-Anhalt, a centre of the mining industry on the eastern flank of the Harz. Copper ore had been mined in neighbouring Mansfeld since the Middle Ages, and the German cosmographer Sebastian Münster had included a woodcut of a fossil fish found there in his illustrated work of 1550, labelling it 'the fish drawn by nature in slate'.[45] In discussing 'ichthyomorphous' stones from Eisleben,

Thunnus circa fretum Herculeum
seu Gaditanum captus in cuius
superficie apparent Triremes à
natura insculptæ militibus atq
tormentis bellicis præmuniti
Erat latitudine pedum 16 longitudine
pedum 32 die 13 May 1565 innuentus
Teste Joanne virtuoso Hispaniarum Regis
Notario.

53 Inscribed tuna, from Aldrovandi, *Tavole*, Biblioteca Universitaria Bologna.

54 Fossil fish from Eisleben, from Aldrovandi, *Tavole*, Biblioteca
Universitaria Bologna.

Aldrovandi noted how some of the forms to be found in these stones resembled salamanders or serpents so much that 'we should admire the beautiful spectacle of nature at play in these stones, which makes the images of various creatures in them so accurate that they seem to have been drawn with a pencil.' (*MM*, p. 101).

The German naturalist Georg Bauer (also known as Agricola) had noted the existence of forms resembling various species of fish in a book on fossils from 1546, but the lack of illustrations in that work was a serious obstacle to their identification. It was the work of Gessner, and the more comprehensive publication of Aldrovandi, that sought to remedy that defect, although by the time Aldrovandi's compilation saw the light of day in 1648, his crude woodcuts were no match for the copperplate engravings of Fabio Colonna's work on stones and fossils that had appeared more than thirty years earlier.

The word 'fossil' originally simply referred to something that had been dug up from the earth. Aldrovandi's *Vomeropsis* fish fossil was found in an Italian location in the Monti Lessini to the northeast of Verona, Bolca, a site that also yielded a rich crop of plant fossils, many of them resembling vegetation found in tropical waters today. Dating from some 50 million years ago, the more than three hundred fish fossils found there make Bolca one of the richest deposits in the world. Given the concentration of so many fossil finds in the territory of Verona – for example, the famous pink stone of Veronese architecture is rich in ammonites – it is not surprising that a lively debate arose among the local scientific community of naturalists, physicians and various members of the aristocratic della Torre family.[46]

The earliest mention of the discovery of fossils in Bolca is in a letter from Pietro Andrea Mattioli, who wrote in 1555:

> I remember being shown by Don Diego [H]urtado de Mendoza, at that time the imperial ambassador in Venice,

some slabs of stone that had been brought from the district of Verona, in which (if they are split in two) various fish species can be found in every detail converted into stone. He declared that an infinite number of them could be found where they had been excavated, so grand and marvellous are the works of nature.[47]

The scholar, bibliophile, mathematician, philosopher, poet and soldier Diego Hurtado de Mendoza was the ambassador of Charles V in Venice from 1539 to 1547, followed by a posting in Rome; he also represented the Holy Roman Emperor at the Council of Trent. It was during his fifteen years spent in Italy that he and a number of associates conducted field expeditions in the Italian countryside to collect plants and minerals, though Mattioli does not state that the Bolca fossils had been collected by Hurtado de Mendoza himself.

Hardly imagining that the fish species found 800 metres (2,625 ft) above sea level in Bolca had once inhabited the edge of a vast sea known by geologists today as the Tethys Ocean before volcanic action caused the extrusion of the sea bottom, Mattioli supposed that, like certain molluscs that had been found alive in the rock, the slabs were evidence that fish could also live in that environment. Girolamo Fracastoro, another of the scholars in the circle of Hurtado de Mendoza, official physician to the Council of Trent and a former pupil of Girolamo della Torre, had asserted their organic origin as early as 1517 on the basis of the fossil shells and crabs that he found in Verona. But after he had been presented with a fossil crab excavated from one of the hills around Verona, the hilltop location of many fossils far from the sea became an obstacle to acceptance of his theory. His attempt to explain the mountaintops on which these traces of maritime species were found as the result of millennia of action by waves in piling up sediment looks quite modern, particularly in the refusal to accept an explanation based on the biblical Flood, but failed to convince everyone. The Flemish physician to the court of Charles V, Jan Van Gorp, who had seen Bolca fossils in the collection of Andrea Loredan in Venice and conducted considerable *in situ* examination of the mountains north of Trent, was unwilling to accept the deep time thesis that Fracastoro's theory entailed or his wave mechanism. Van Gorp supposed that some moisture found both in the sea and in rock could engender living beings in stone. It was the argument of the Flemish physician that convinced Aldrovandi/Ambrosini, who cited from Van Gorp's 1569 *Origines Antwerpianae* in the *Musaeum metallicum* (MM, p. 820).[48]

These fish and plant fossils are examples of the type known as the trace fossil. What is preserved in stone is not the remains of the animal or plant, but an imprint left by its physical form before its dissolution. The stone therefore comes to resemble the shape visible inside a woodblock that has been engraved for printing. Body fossils, on the other hand, are the fossilized remains that have undergone mineralization or chemical change, such as the two fossilized shark's teeth (*glossopetrae*) taken by Mary Stuart when she returned to Scotland to rule as its queen; they are listed in her inventory as 'langues de serpentz' and were believed by André Thevet and others to be antidotes to poison.[49] Among the various 'petrified shells' included in the *Musaeum metallicum* are shells that have been petrified and trace fossils, the concave imprint left on a stone by a shell (MM, pp. 823ff). Aldrovandi was aware of the nature of the body fossil type, accepting its organic origin and attributing the conversion into stone to the agency of a petrifying fluid.

During his stay as a 27-year-old in Rome, he had admired a petrified elephant's jaw in one of the Roman collections and it was an interest that was to remain throughout his active life (ANT, p. 190). In 1557 Mattioli sent him a piece of a petrified pine tree with bark that had been found deep in the rock of a mountain in Bohemia, and puzzled over how a tree could have reached so far down into the living rock of a silver mine.[50] Decades later, during Aldrovandi's visit to Florence in 1586, among the wonders observed in the collection of Giuseppe Casabona he admired a 'piece of alcyonium [a soft coral also known as dead man's fingers] like a sponge, resembling a Turkish turban through a sport of nature (*lusu naturae*)'.[51] Although the category of fossils and minerals is rather under-represented in the collection of coloured drawings, they constituted a significant part of his collection of objects and are abundantly cited in the *Musaeum metallicum*. In his circle of acquaintances, Francesco Calzolari and Michele Mercati were among those who could supply him with such items as fossilized nautilus shells. In 1571 Calzolari asked him for some rare mineral from his 'copious and well-stocked *studio*', indicating that Aldrovandi's collection was already considerable.[52] At the beginning of his friendship with Francesco de' Medici, Aldrovandi wrote to Alberto Bolognetti with the offer to dedicate to the Grand Duke one of his writings, 'in each of which will be revealed many fine secrets of nature, and properties that arise from the form of those animate and inanimate mixtures'.[53]

55 Alabaster sheet with river-like markings, from Aldrovandi, *Musaeum metallicum in libros III distributum* (1648).
56 Tree-like branching structure of dendrite, from Aldrovandi, *Musaeum metallicum*.

In the house of Niccolò Gaddi in Florence he admired the 'petrified part of the head of some animal' and 'wood that has been transformed into a jasper-like stony material so that it is not easy to distinguish it from jasper stone', as well as 'a quadran-gular slab of marble variegated by nature with many decorations'.[54] He returned to the theme in his *Musaeum metallicum* with such woodcut images as a sheet of alabaster 'imitating a river with its markings' (illus. 55). Italian artists like the Florentine Antonio Tempesta made use of the properties of these *lapides figurati* in scenes such as Moses striking water from the rock or the crossing of the Red Sea to paint compositions in which it is often difficult for the naked eye to distinguish between ground and painted surface. Aldrovandi was aware of and illustrated a sample of dendrite, a stone with a branching structure that displays 'such elegant groves that no painter could depict them better and more elegantly with a brush' (illus. 56). This property meant that the stone could be deployed in landscapes in which the natural mark-ings of the stone suggested the form of trees. The artistic results were the product of the active collaboration between the capacity of nature to form images and the creativity of the artist.[55]

SIX

Art and Artists

ainting, portrait, drawing – whenever it proved difficult or impossible to transport an object within the
network of Aldrovandi and his correspondents, all
were aware that what could not be present 'in person' would
have to be conveyed by means of a representation. As he wrote
to Cardinal Gabriele Paleotti in 1581:

> Experience shows how useful the paintings of various
> animals are to scientists . . . as can be seen in my Histories
> and in my images, where I have painted from life three
> thousand different animals. The combination of these
> paintings with the histories enables scientists to arrive at
> full cognition of those which were known to the ancients.
> It is impossible to imagine anything more useful, because
> if the ancients had had painted portraits made of all the
> things that they have described, we would not find so
> many doubts and countless errors among the writers.[1]

Elsewhere Aldrovandi affirmed that an image was indispensable
if a description of an object from the natural world were to have
any demonstrative validity. Otherwise, the textual description
would be quite useless – anticipating one of the fundamental
principles that guided the activities of the Lincean Academy in
Rome.[2] This was nothing new; when faced with the limitations

of verbal descriptions when it came to explaining the novelties of tropical flora to a European audience, the first author to write a natural history of the New World, Gonzalo Fernández de Oviedo, had recommended visual representation: 'It should rather be painted by the hand of Berruguete or another excellent painter like him, or by that of Leonardo da Vinci or Andrea Mantegna, famous painters whom I knew in Italy.'[3] For the same reason, Aldrovandi's planned expeditionary force to the New World would have included painters as well as writers.

A two-dimensional image would serve as a substitute for the absent three-dimensional object that it represented. In Florence, Aldrovandi saw a painting of a dusky white and scaly rhinoceros – hardly an animal that one could keep in a private collection – in the collection of Raffaele Bondelmonti, but he also had genuine rhinoceros parts: a number of horns, a tooth and even some dark coagulated blood. Together, the present parts and the image of the absent beast were intended to conjure up a mental picture in which the parts and the whole were integrated.[4]

In October 1561 Stefano Rosselli in Florence received a live bird, of which he gave Aldrovandi a verbal description. After Aldrovandi had replied with comments regarding the identification, Rosselli added that the bird 'is extremely tame and enjoys being touched and in company, but when left alone it squawks and makes it clear that it wants to follow the person who was with it'. He promised to have an accurate painting made of it, and when it died to have it preserved and to send the specimen to Aldrovandi.[5] Earlier in the same year he had had a painting of a crow made for Aldrovandi, but its head was somehow torn, so he had another one made and dispatched, along with the promise to send the bird itself if desired.[6] Live bird, painting, dead specimen: they are all a part of the world of the collectors.

In February 1565 Rosselli wrote to Aldrovandi that he had taken the latter's painter to portray lions – the official animal of Florence – but had not heard since whether he had been successful or not. Rosselli himself, he went on, had ordered one of his artists to make drawings of a lion and a lioness, which he wanted to send Aldrovandi after they had been coloured. The carnival festivities made that impossible, so he decided to send them as they were, praising their accuracy, although the lioness had turned out smaller than the lion.[7] Later in the same year, difficulties of a different kind arose. Rosselli was reported by another botanist, Sebastiano Soavi, to be on the point of sending Aldrovandi a portrait of a lion and a lioness:

> He would have already sent them, but for experiencing such difficulty in having them painted because they move around so much when they are on their feet, and the rest of the time they are together, so then he decided to paint them together, but then he did not know the size of the paper.[8]

Artists had grappled with the difficulty of representing lions for years. Albrecht Dürer's watercolour of a lion in front of a cave from the end of the fifteenth century shows the disproportionate animal in an artificial pose; by 1521 he was more successful when he was able to draw a lion in the imperial menagerie in Ghent from life.[9] Years later, when Peter Paul Rubens needed to paint lions, as in his *Daniel in the Lion's Den*, he ran up against the same problem. In his case he solved it by combining detailed study drawings based on Italian sculptures with added colour and texture derived from the observation of live lions.[10]

Ferrante Imperato in Naples had received a rare and beautiful globe fish in 1572, but it slipped from his hand while he was holding it, so it was a representation of it, not the specimen itself, that he was obliged to send to Aldrovandi together with the suggestion that it might be called a marine porcupine.[11] (Aldrovandi seems to have liked the idea, because when he visited the collection of Giuseppe Casabona in 1586, he called the first item in his list a marine porcupine (*Istrix marinus*).)[12] This example should serve as a reminder that when Aldrovandi collected images, it was not always from a desire to give primacy to the visual. Just as he depended on his wide network to obtain objects from far-flung regions that were beyond his own reach but were essential to his encyclopaedic project, so he depended on a supply of images to remedy the gaps in his collection in the case of animals, plants or minerals that for practical reasons, or just because someone dropped one, did not make it on to the shelves of his collection, but would still deserve a place in the projected encyclopaedic publications.

Images were, at least in theory, a substitute for the real thing, and therefore less preferable where alternatives were present. When in 1560 Aldrovandi sent Mattioli both a lotus branch and a painting of what he regarded as the same plant, Mattioli was not convinced.[13] At times, though, Aldrovandi seems to have been indifferent to whether an item was physically present or only an image. When he lists more than thirty fish in the collection of Jacopo Ligozzi, he mentions successively two fish 'like mine', followed immediately by a third, a catfish, 'like my painting of one'.[14] Here the painting has the same evidential status as the objects themselves.

The same is true of the display of Aldrovandi's collection itself. In the first of the rooms dedicated to showing his coloured drawings and woodblocks, two paintings of unicorn horns, one from the Duke of Mantua and one from Poland, were suspended from the central beam of the ceiling. Aldrovandi may have requested these copies from one of the painters working in the Mantuan court, such as Teodoro Ghisi. And the doorway area that opened on to the largest room, where most of the *naturalia* were exhibited, included both three-dimensional objects such as a stuffed stork and a two-dimensional painting of a beaver. Once again, actual objects and representations of other objects appear to rub shoulders without any suggestion of hierarchy or precedence.[15] In this respect the practice of the Grand Duke of Tuscany was no different from that of the Bolognese naturalist. After describing a number of *naturalia* seen in the Medici palace in Florence during his 1577 visit, Aldrovandi's list continued 'besides these *naturalia*, I also saw some paintings in the museum of the duke' and went on to name eight paintings of *naturalia*.[16]

Both men employed painters, though Aldrovandi sometimes complained that his own painter was ill or out of town working on other commissions. Nor was he as talented as the Grand Duke's painter: when Aldrovandi sent Francesco three paintings of plants and another three of animals in 1581, he added that, if they were not to Francesco's taste, the Grand Duke could have copies made by his own 'diligent' painter.[17] Yet what Aldrovandi's painter may have lacked in talent he made up for in terms of productivity. In Aldrovandi's employ for more than thirty years, Giovanni Neri produced a substantial number of images for him.[18] Aldrovandi was in something of a quandary: he was well aware that Neri was not a top-class artist, but since the quality of his production reflected on the status of Aldrovandi's project, he was reluctant to denigrate him in public. The two men later had a falling out over Neri's supplying of images to other clients, given the high premium that Aldrovandi placed on the originality of his works.

In the era of manual reproduction of the work of art, the standard practice was to send a (coloured) drawing to a corre-spondent, who would have a copy made and then return the original, but not all exchanges were of this simple kind. Inevitably, this entailed a wide range in the quality of the images that the artists produced. The woodcut of a 'many-horned stag' featured in the *Monstrorum historia* (illus. 57) has been shown to be an exact copy of a coloured drawing by Hans Hoffmann made

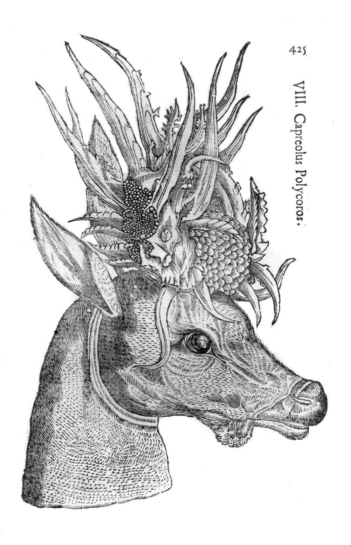

57 Many-horned stag, after Hans Hoffmann, from Aldrovandi, *Monstrorum historia* (1642).

58 Arcimboldo, African duiker and American coati, from Aldrovandi, *Tavole*, Biblioteca Universitaria Bologna.

for the Rudolfine court in Prague in 1589.[19] The superb quality of the draughtsmanship is matched by the use of a high-status support, parchment, as was fitting for a work that was intended to be given a place in the Kunstkammer of Rudolf II. Another prominent artist connected with Prague and whose work is included among the painted drawings of Aldrovandi is Giuseppe Arcimboldo, who was active in the Rudolfine court in a similar capacity to that exercised by Jacopo Ligozzi in the Medici court in Florence. Through the intermediary of the physician Franciscus de Paduanis, probably a former medical student of Aldrovandi in Bologna who was employed at the imperial court, Aldrovandi received paintings of five exotic animals by Arcimboldo, including an African duiker and an American coati (illus. 58).[20] He was less fortunate in the case of a rare plant from Hungary known as the Persian lily: de Paduanis asked Arcimboldo to make a painting of it for his Bolognese friend, but while the Milanese artist was away for several days to attend a wedding, the condition of the plant deteriorated to such an extent that Aldrovandi had to be content with a verbal description alone.[21] On another occasion,

59 Syrian cat with mouse and fruit, from Aldrovandi, *Tavole*, Biblioteca Universitaria Bologna.

when he asked the naturalist and specialist on herbs Ippolito Geniforti della Sirena to send him some paintings from Mantua, including those of a stag and a unicorn, he was told that there would be some delay because the young painter 'a little given to fantasy' employed by Ippolito had just begun to decorate the facade of his house.[22]

Aldrovandi allowed other artists to make use of his paintings too. Writing to Cardinal Paleotti in late 1581 about two well-known artists who had died in the previous five years, he wrote: 'I remember the late Bolognese Lorenzino [Sabatini] and Samachino [Orazio Samacchini], who were perfect in their day, but nevertheless, when they needed to paint some plant or animal in one of their histories, they came to me and copied the paintings that my painter had made.'[23] Since Aldrovandi solicited and received images from a very wide network of correspondents, there was no standard format. Some depict a plant species devoid of any context, while others include other details and may even go so far as to feature a narrative. Sometimes the whole sheet is coloured

60 Syrian cat, from Aldrovandi, *De quadrupedibus digitatis viviparis* (1645).

in using either tempera or watercolour, accommodating the object(s) within the context of a landscape or human occupation. Birds might be depicted with their favourite food – say a frog or a worm – dangling from their beak. A frontally gazing cat seems oblivious to the mouse behind it that is heading for some ripe red cherries, though Aldrovandi probably found this too anecdotal for a scientific image because the woodblock cut for printing omits these accessories (illus. 59 and 60).[24] Quadrupeds might be placed on a patch of land with vegetation like an island on the page; a drawing of a stick insect by Agostino Carracci sent to Aldrovandi from Rome by Pietro Stefanoni in January 1599 sets the elongated insect on a strip of land with stones and grass to show its horizontal mode of locomotion.[25] There might be annotation or a date.

We can gain a better idea of the circulation of multiple copies at this time from the case of eleven paintings of Mexican trees that were included among the coloured drawings of plants in the painted herbal compiled by Pier'Antonio Michiel in Venice. Michiel was just as much at the mercy of the suppliers of his images as Aldrovandi, and his 1,028 coloured drawings of plants by a variety of hands display considerable stylistic variation. These eleven images were the result of two successive copying operations, based on original paintings done in 'India' and taken to the court of Charles V. A first set of copies was made for Marcantonio Da Mula, the Venetian ambassador at the Spanish court. A second set of copies was made from Da Mula's copies, and it is these images – copies of copies – that we find in Michiel's herbal. But there are more: four coloured drawings in the Aldrovandi collection closely match four of the images in Michiel's painted herbal (illus. 61; see also illus. 17), but Aldrovandi's images are not direct copies of Michiel's and they reached him by a different route, as a letter to Francesco de' Medici from September 1577 makes clear:

Cucumis arboreus
Hulxio Hispanis
Pepinæ fructui Hispanis
dicco similis.

61 *Cucumis arboreus* (candle tree), from Aldrovandi, *Tavole*, Biblioteca
Universitaria Bologna.

Together with this box, I send you four figures of four
very beautiful and strange Indian plants, which I received
from Portugal eight years ago and had painted from
these originals in my histories; Your Highness will be
able to have your excellent painter paint them, who will
be able to improve on them and make them more beautiful and perfect. Your Highness is requested to keep
these originals, because I have had them copied in my
histories.[26]

In a long digression on the list of items that Aldrovandi sent
to the Grand Duke on that occasion, he compares Francesco's
passion for knowledge about the natural world with the interest
of antiquarians in portraits of the illustrious men and women
of the past. Coins and medals were already being used as the
basis for such portraits in the Middle Ages, but it was not until
the beginning of the sixteenth century that the antiquarian
Andrea Fulvio published more than two hundred of them in
his *Illustrium imagines* of 1517, to be followed by the compilations
of Guillaume Rouillé and others later in the century. It is publications like these that Aldrovandi had in mind when he wrote:

If the knowledge of ancient medals is such a delight and
entertainment for princes and other fine intellects, who
does not know how Your Highness vastly surpasses not
just the moderns, but all the antiquarians of Europe in
this field; you have collected every kind of them in gold,
silver and metal, the select, ancient and rarest that can
be imagined and found, and assembled them with great
order. In truth, their value is an inestimable treasure just
from putting before our eyes the true likeness of those
great Emperors and Princes of old for their magnani-
mous deeds. Those Princes can no longer be found in

nature, nor is it possible to verify whether they are an individual and correct likeness.

The science and knowledge of painting plants and animals far surpasses that of medals, because in this particular cognition of paintings the species can be verified, which are eternal according to the philosophers. It is they, not the particulars, that constitute the true science.

The passage is provocative, because it represents an attempt to put the study of nature on a par with, if not above, the study of antiquity, which enjoyed a high standing among the humanists. Moreover, it was a useful science, because in linking an accurate painting with a verbal description of the plant or animal in question, covering its nature, habitat and its manifest and latent properties, the whole was 'directed toward human benefit and use'.[27]

Stefano Rosselli was an experienced botanist who had engaged in numerous field expeditions with Luigi Leoni, and his study and preparation of medicinal plants was praised in similar terms to Aldrovandi's eulogy of Francesco for its benefits for the health of the people of Florence, where his well-stocked garden and apothecary were situated. His nephew later wrote of him:

After having conducted many study trips in the mountains of Pistoia and the Apennines in his youth in the company of learned men whom he took with him at his own expense, he also ordered many rare and exotic *naturalia* from remote parts and with great effort to obtain cognition of them; and many medicinal plants and herbs that are unknown in this region of ours, with which he filled a garden that he had attached to his villa . . . This prompted him to have many simples painted accurately from life on imperial paper.[28]

Rosselli modelled his garden and collection on those of
Aldrovandi, with whom he was on cordial terms. His employment of a team of artists to produce images for Aldrovandi when
requested testifies to his importance for the latter's ever expand-
ing image collection, even though in 1567 Rosselli felt able to
write: 'I would not know what to send you for your museum,
which is by now so copious that it is impossible to send anything
that is not already familiar.'[29]

LIGOZZI

Another collector who was eager to obtain either objects or
images of them was Calzolari in Verona. When he asked Aldrovandi for two plants, a sneezewort and a scilla, he stated that he
would be happy to receive drawings of them if the plants themselves were not forthcoming.[30] That Calzolari was collecting
images of *naturalia* as well as the objects themselves also emerges
from a long letter to Aldrovandi from the end of 1571, in which
he mentioned an artist in Verona who had painted simples and
fish for the herbalist and collector Leone Tartaglini in Venice
that were marvellously lifelike and recommended his services to
Aldrovandi.[31] A few days later he returned to the subject in asking
Aldrovandi for a painting of some parrots by his – Aldrovandi's
– painter, promising in return to send a sample of the Veronese
painter's work.[32]

This Veronese painter has been identified with Jacopo Ligozzi,
who must have been about 21 years old at the time. Little is known
about his youth and training, except that he came from a family
of artists who worked in princely courts in northern Italy. A series
of frescoes once in the Casa Fumanelli in Santa Maria in Organo,
Verona, has been attributed to the collaboration of the young
Jacopo with his father, Giovanni Ermanno Ligozzi. Interestingly,
it portrays the cavalcade of Pope Clement VII and Charles V in

Bologna, an event that was the talk of the town when Aldrovandi was just a boy.

Born around 1549, by 1575 at the latest Jacopo had entered the service of the Medici court as an all-round artist on a generous salary (second only to that of the sculptor Giambologna). Besides his precise renderings of objects of natural history, he was expected to design the decorations and costumes for spectacles and celebrations, jewels, lamps, ornamental vases, furniture, carriages, even the decoration of a telescope for Galileo. In this respect he was following in his family's footsteps going back to his grandparents. His grandfather had worked for Emperor Maximilian in Milan, and a great-uncle had been in the service of Prince Bishop Cles in Trent.[33]

He first appears in the Aldrovandi correspondence during the Bolognese naturalist's visit to Florence in June 1577, when he saw 'all the paintings done from life by Jacomo Ligozzi, which lack nothing but the breath of life'.[34] More details emerge from his second visit in June 1586, when among the sites he visited was the Medici Villa di Pratolino, where he marvelled at Giambologna's 10-metre-tall (33 ft) statue of *The Apennine* that had been completed only a few years earlier, but he was equally impressed by the fountain of Thetis situated behind it. After admiring the ingenious use of shells in its construction and the feat of engineering that produced the myriad jets of water, he went on to describe its painted decoration:

> Around the walls on the sides of the fountain are painted the island of Elba with the fish that are caught in its waters, depicted so exactly that they seem to be breathing, done by the excellent Iacobo Ligozzi *from his own specimens*. On the other wall is painted the city of Livorno with the fish that inhabit those waters, painted with consummate skill.[35]

Besides preserved specimens of fish, Ligozzi also had a few stuffed fowl, a petrified fungus and a live mongoose,[36] but it is as an artist rather than a collector that he has gone down in history. Aldrovandi's comment brings out the intrinsic link between specimen and painting, as several of the fish listed in Ligozzi's collection are explicitly connected with Elba or Livorno. Aldrovandi's judgement is borne out by the testimony of the Dominican professor Agostino del Riccio, who wrote an unpublished manuscript on stones ('Libro delle pietre'), including the precious stones that the Medici were quarrying to use in their decorative and architectural projects. Another of del Riccio's works, 'Giardino di un re', contains recommendations on how to lay out a garden fit for a king. When he comes to a grotto representing the techniques for catching large and small fish, he cites the example of the Pratolino, 'painted by the excellent painter Iacopo Ligozzi, with whom I am on very friendly terms'. Del Riccio adds that the purpose of such compositions was to delight all those foreigners who have not seen so many types of fish painted. The paintings were thus substitutes for direct observation of the fish themselves, and therefore had epistemological as well as aesthetic value.[37]

Although the paintings themselves have not survived, there is a pen and ink drawing by Ligozzi of a view looking towards the island of Elba in which a fisherman occupies the foreground, while the festoons hanging above the scene like a curtain are composed of fishing nets full of fish and a cluster of fish hangs vertically from the centre as a lively variation on the usual curtain tassel. Another pen and ink drawing, this time of the harbour of Portoferraio on Elba, may also be connected with the paintings.[38]

Besides fish, Ligozzi was noted for his extremely accurate depiction of plants.[39] When Andrea Cesalpino, director of the botanical garden in Padua, published his *De plantis* in 1583, he regretted in the dedication to Francesco de' Medici that he had not been able to include images taken from those in the collection of the Grand Duke, 'painted with such precision that they express even the most minute differences'.[40] It was the same meticulous attention to the particular features of each plant that much later secured Ligozzi the commission to illustrate the botanical species contained in the Farnese gardens on the Palatine Hill in Rome for a 1625 publication by one of Cesalpino's students, Pietro Castelli.[41] The extreme level of exactness advertised in the title had to be borne out by the painstaking accuracy of the designer of those prints.

There is a famous story about the rivalry between the Greek painters Parrhasius and Zeuxis in which the latter made a painting of grapes that were so realistic that birds tried to eat them. Aldrovandi gave it a feline twist when he wrote about a painting by Ligozzi of a cat that was so lifelike that it provoked dogs to attack it, as well as similarly deceiving visitors to the room in which it was displayed.[42] As the image has not survived, we cannot tell whether the story is an invention of Aldrovandi to suggest that Ligozzi was as talented as Zeuxis, or whether it really existed, but either way it is eloquent testimony to the association of the name Ligozzi with almost photographic realism.

While working for the Medici court, Ligozzi was also given various commissions by the Florentine nobleman Niccolò Gaddi, whose collecting tastes rivalled those of Francesco de' Medici. Aldrovandi visited his collection during that memorable 1586 trip to Florence, noting the presence of exquisitely crafted *pietra dura* tables, Chinese woven silk, a rhinoceros hoof and tooth, plants, fish, an Egyptian urn with hieroglyphs, petrified wood – in short, a collection very like Aldrovandi's own.[43] Gaddi was also interested in architecture, so the view of Portoferraio with its fortifications may have been intended for him. Though Ligozzi did not work solely for Francesco de' Medici, he was in the exclusive service of the court and was not expected to take on outside commissions. Obviously, Gaddi was close enough to Medici circles to be regarded as an insider.

So was Aldrovandi. His requests for copies of paintings of plants, mammals, birds and fish were always received favourably by Francesco de' Medici, and the flow of images from Florence to Bologna continued under Francesco's successor Ferdinando. Not all these images were done by Jacopo Ligozzi; Aldrovandi only had around thirty done by the artist, his younger brother Francesco or a cousin.[44] Each court or prestigious garden tended to attract a circle of painters of *naturalia*: in Venice, for example, Pier'Antonio Michiel could count on the Venetian painter Domenico dalle Greche for some of the images in his painted herbal, while Daniele Barbaro had 'a certain master Pliny' to make images of fish for him, some of which ended up in Aldrovandi's hands.[45] If we add the copyists and imitators, it becomes clear that the authorship of a particular drawing or painting is hard to establish, except in the case of a handful of Ligozzi images containing his monogram, cunningly concealed in miniature between the legs of an elk, because a court painter was not supposed to sign his works (see illus. 15).

The much sparser correspondence between Aldrovandi and the successor to Francesco de' Medici, his brother Ferdinando, reveals little of the cordiality that existed between the naturalist and Francesco. The obsequious requests for support for his vast publishing endeavours and for further material (a vulture, or the plants for which Giuseppe Casabona had spent an entire year botanizing on Crete) are accompanied by the dispatch of the three volumes of his work on ornithology and a volume on insects that were appearing between 1599 and 1603.[46] Similar concerns emerge from a letter of February 1602 to the young French scholar Nicolas-Claude Fabri de Peiresc, whom Aldrovandi had met in Bologna during the Italian journey of the Peiresc brothers in 1600.[47] Aldrovandi complains that he has had great difficulty in finding a suitable painter because of Carnival, but manages to send Peiresc a copy of an image of a flamingo, probably taken from the one in preparation for printing in the third volume of his *Ornithologia*.[48]

Ferdinando continued the botanical gardens of his predecessor and in doing so he made much use of the Flemish botanist Jodocus De Goethuysen, alias Giuseppe Casabona, whose presence in Florence is already documented from 1571. From 1586 to 1593 he was in charge of reorganizing the garden of simples in Florence, which was situated close to the workplace of Jacopo Ligozzi. During this period Francesco sent Casabona to Crete, where he came across a German artist, Georg Dyckmann, who agreed to portray from life the plants that Casabona collected on the island. Dyckmann's skilfully painted illustrations of Cretan plants are now in the Pisa University Library. Some copies of them have been found among the painted images in Aldrovandi's collection, but it is unclear whether these copies were made by Dyckmann or, more probably, by another copyist.[49]

When Casabona was put in charge of the botanical garden in Pisa, he employed several artists to portray all the simples and rare plants with the assistance of the German artist Daniel Froeschl from the wealthy city of Augsburg. Northern artists were particularly appreciated as miniaturists capable of representing specimens of the natural world in all their detail, and the Augsburg goldsmiths and silversmiths were famous for the delicacy and precision of their work. Moreover, as the city where Emperor Maximilian's Imperial Council had been situated, it had a rich tradition of artistic print commissions and could boast such artists as Hans Weiditz, whose watercolours were used for the woodcuts in Otto Brunfels's herbal in the 1530s.

A no longer extant album of 258 folios containing 2,000 images of plants and flowers 'marvellously painted from life' and signed by 'D. F. Augustanus' was presumably made by the German artist for the Grand Duke, while another florilegium, the Codice

Casabona, which is now in the Pisa University Library, contains accurate representations of 414 plants from the Pisan botanical garden, including the prestigious tulip. Froeschl continued to work for the Medici until 1604, when he went to the court of Rudolf II in Prague to supervise his collections. From there he used his skill as a botanical painter to make designs that were then sent, together with the requisite precious stones, to Florence to be transformed into *pietra dura* tables, an activity to which Jacopo Ligozzi also contributed. It is therefore quite justifiable to speak of an artistic workshop in this case.[50]

Froeschl's activity was not confined to botanical illustration alone: in a letter to Aldrovandi from 1599, Francesco Malocchi, the successor of Giuseppe Casabona in Pisa, wrote that he was sending 'two birds miniated by that most excellent miniaturist Daniel Froeschl of Augsburg, which His Highness has received from the islands of Capo Verde, an Indian region, one alive and the other dead'.[51] Aldrovandi already had a coloured drawing of the Brazilian tanager,[52] but that one was copied directly from Pierre Belon's inaccurate woodcut image of the bird taken from a dead specimen. He must have been delighted to receive a more up-to-date version (Belon's book on birds was published in 1555). While the cardinal was still alive, the 1599 specimen of a tanager was just as dead on arrival as Belon's model had been. Moreover, as the specimen had arrived without feet, Aldrovandi was uncertain whether it should be identified with Belon's tanager. He therefore created a separate category, the 'footless Indian blackbird'. The vivid red colouring of Froeschl's painting of the two birds (illus. 62) evoked the association of Brazil with redwood. Aldrovandi used Froeschl's image of the two birds, with due acknowledgement, in the second volume of his *Ornithology* (illus. 63). While the live cardinal perched on a branch presented no problems, the footless tanager is shown hovering awkwardly above a plant on the ground.[53]

62 Daniel Froeschl, cardinal and tanager, from Aldrovandi, *Tavole*, Biblioteca Universitaria Bologna.

Before the age of colour printing, woodcuts could be coloured by hand, as in the case of a copy of Belon in the Bibliothèque national de France, the hand-coloured copies of Aldrovandi's *Ornithología* sent to Duke Francesco Maria II of Urbino and the Cardinal of Bologna, or the copy of Aldrovandi's work on fishes in the dal Pozzo library, where it was accompanied by a hand-coloured edition of Mattioli as well.[54] However, the accuracy of the colouring was not always guaranteed. For example, a number of copies of the commentary on Dioscorides by Mattioli contained hand-coloured woodcuts, but Aldrovandi, as he wrote to Cardinal Paleotti in 1581, was not satisfied:

> Many today have wished to colour the plants delineated and printed by Mattioli, and through not having had the green plant in front of them, they have made many blunders by having painted all the plants in that book in the same green colour. Nevertheless, the variety of colours is infinite . . . and although generally speaking most plants are green, there is an infinite diversity in those same colours, some dark greens tending towards black, other light greens tending towards blue, others to crimson, others to dark grey, others to ochre.

63 Footless tanager, from Aldrovandi, *Ornithologiae tomus alter* (1600).

Mattioli, in turn, complained about the inaccuracy of the copies of plants made for him by Aldrovandi's artist. Aldrovandi continued in the same letter to Paleotti: 'So if you want to paint plants naturally, you need not only a very skilful painter, but even more you need to have the plant freshly plucked from the ground, because dried plants cannot be painted.'[55] Repeating the advice of Dioscorides, he added that each different stage in the growth of the plant was to be represented, even if the stage of flowering was the most important because it facilitated identification.

Following Aristotle, Aldrovandi considered colour to be a secondary, accidental characteristic of things that was nevertheless essential to a proper cognition of them. Among his manuscripts are excerpts on the topic of colour referring to existing treatises, but these are exercises in nomenclature rather than of much practical use. Lists of colour terms in different languages may serve a lexicological purpose, but are not helpful to the natural historian. Moreover, to define a colour term as the colour of chicory or of a hare is, in actual fact, not very useful, and to define the terms in relation to objects, given the variety in the hues of different objects, such as the greens mentioned above, is not very useful either. Here, Aldrovandi's book learning and love of classification seem to have got the better of his interest in direct observation of the natural world.

THE SUBURBAN VILLA

Aldrovandi employed several different artists for the decoration of his suburban villa in Sant'Antonio di Savena, located at the time outside the eastern portal (Porta San Vitale) of the outer walls of Bologna.[56] He purchased it as an investment with the dowry of his second wife, Francesca Fontana, soon after their marriage in 1565. Around ten years later, Aldrovandi began to compose drafts of an iconographic programme for the interior decoration that show him weighing up various possibilities before settling on the definitive one. They are all the material we have regarding the decoration, as the villa was demolished for the construction of the rail link between Bologna and Ancona in the nineteenth century.

While the scenes from the *Odyssey* painted two decades earlier by Pellegrino Tibaldi in Palazzo Poggi do not display a programme, Aldrovandi characteristically laid down in great detail the instructions for his painter. These were drawn up by a certain Alessandro Bordini, a teacher of mathematics and amanuensis of Aldrovandi for many years, about whom nothing further is known at present. Aldrovandi's painter was to depict 24 scenes in chronological order, from the feigned madness of Ulysses to avoid leaving Ithaca for the Trojan War to his death at the hands of Telegonos, son of Ulysses and Circe. Aldrovandi's richly stocked library contained various editions of Homer, including an illustrated Italian version from 1582, while for the non-Homeric episodes that opened and closed the sequence he used the *Bellum Troianum* composed by Lucius Septimius and supposed to derive from a Greek original attributed to Dictys of Crete. He was also able to draw on sixteenth-century mythological compilations such as that by Natale Conti, of which he certainly owned a copy.

Although, as we have seen, Aldrovandi was hardly an antiquarian, he was well read in the classics and specified details such as the hair colour and complexion of the various figures or the colour of their clothes, but – not surprisingly – it was on the correct representation of animals and plants that he laid particular emphasis. For instance, the episode of the Lotus Eaters gave him an opportunity to explain that a lotus tree is similar to a pear tree. Each scene or group of scenes was accompanied by two lines of verse summarizing the action. It is characteristic of Aldrovandi

– who, unlike most of his contemporaries, considered writing to be older than painting – that, instead of allowing the images to narrate a story, he feels the need to tell it in words in case the visitor might not be able to identify each of the scenes.[57]

A further three rooms were decorated by the Bolognese min-iaturist Cerva and his son with emblems on the walls. This was an unusual feature, as the more common practice was to place emblems between the wooden panelling of the ceiling. We may suppose that here too Aldrovandi had a didactic purpose in mind that went beyond mere decoration, for if visitors to the villa were to ponder on the significance of one or more emblems, they would not have wanted to have to crane their necks to observe them in the ceiling.

The emblems, all of which were taken from previous compil-ations, were distributed over the three rooms: thirteen in the first and twelve in each of the other two. The majority were accompanied by one or more animals, three by plants. The animals were distributed by category: birds in the first room, combined with emblems that have a match in the Aldrovandian volumes on ornithology; quadrupeds in the third; and a mixture of species in the second, including a harpy, a chimaera and a two-footed dog, all present in the pages of the posthumous publication on mon-sters. Besides these correspondences between the fauna and flora accompanying the emblems and the publications, almost all of them can be found in Aldrovandi's collection of coloured draw-ings. Moreover, we have already come across some of them as items in the collection housed in Aldrovandi's museum in the city, such as the alcion set in the doorway of the largest of its rooms.

The tranquillity of this bird that built its nest in the sea made it an attractive emblem for the artistic connoisseur Monsignor Giovanni Battista Agucchi, one of Aldrovandi's Bolognese cor-respondents, who wrote in 1602 that he was eager to obtain all three volumes of the naturalist's work on ornithology to help in devising appropriate devices for himself. When the third volume, in which Aldrovandi discusses the alcion, appeared the following year, Agucchi seized upon the passage in which the author cited Aristotle and Pliny for the fact that the alcion's nest was made of the spikes of a fish that were called *agucchia*. To one who had to survive the vicissitudes of life at court (Agucchi was in the service of the Aldobrandini during these years), the notion of halcyon days must indeed have offered a refreshing prospect.[58]

The way in which Agucchi sought to discover emblems that were appropriate to his personal condition mirrors how Aldrovandi conceived the entire decorative programme of the villa as an expression of his own qualities. There were already numerous moralizing interpretations of the figure of Ulysses by this time, and Aldrovandi drew on them to imply his own virtues. The unconventional opening of the series of paintings – of scenes from the life of Ulysses, such as his feigned madness to avoid going to war and leaving Penelope in Ithaca – was in tune with the inscriptions in the villa in praise of family life and the joys of conjugal love. On a less lofty level, at a time when the number of figures in a painting was an index of its value, Aldrovandi's specification that no fewer than 132 figures were to be painted in the scenes was a proud boast of the wealth and status that he had achieved.

This self-presentation continued in the rooms with the emblems. The viper and hellebore – both ingredients of theriac – in the first room, with a motto expressing their ability to both harm and cure, can be read as a scarcely veiled reference to the fame of Aldrovandi's own theriac production. At the centre of the twelve emblems in the second room was the sunflower with the motto *Illustriora sequor* (I pursue the nobler), which Aldrovandi considered appropriate for one whose mind is set on lofty studies and noble enterprises, while other emblems evoked purity, fidelity and concord.

Aldrovandi also made his presence felt in the chapel and in the room of portraits. The altarpiece in the former was done in 1585 by 24-year-old Camillo Procaccini, whom Cardinal Paleotti had contracted to paint scenes from the life of St Peter in the presbytery of Bologna Cathedral. Aldrovandi's altarpiece showed the Virgin in heaven surrounded by the martyr saints who were celebrated on his birthday, 11 September – so here too, at the religious heart of the villa, he was once again at the centre.

The portrait in the small gallery of Aldrovandi's second wife, Francesca, by the Florentine Lorenzo Benini, who worked primarily as a delineator (the intermediary who transfers an image from the drawing to the woodblock for printing) for Aldrovandi from 1585 to 1587, recalls the character of Penelope, for Francesca too is the recipient of conventional praise for her good looks and moral qualities.[59] The distich that accompanies Benini's portrait of the naturalist himself runs: 'This is not your image, Aristotle, but that of Ulysses:/ The features are different, but the intellect (*ingenium*) is the same.' The conceit by which Aldrovandi becomes a second Aristotle, as well as a second Ulysses, was repeated when the same two-line verse was placed beneath the engraving of Aldrovandi aged 74 at the opening of the first volume of the *Ornithology*.[60] These portraits are followed by those of the two main patrons of Aldrovandi, Francesco and Ferdinando de' Medici. The accompanying distichs conventionally underline their greatness, but also imply a self-congratulatory pat on the back for Aldrovandi for having secured such illustrious patrons.

The last two paintings in this room are of a 'hairy girl' and her equally hairy father. The reader has already come across Antonietta and her father, Pedro González, from Tenerife, who both suffered from hypertrichosis. She was kept by the noblewoman Isabella Pallavicino, Marchesa di Soragna, as 'an ornament of her house' in Parma, so it may be that Aldrovandi kept this portrait in the personal collection in his villa rather than in his museum because it combined scientific interest with personal attachment.[61] A small painting in oils on canvas (illus. 64), now in the Musée du Château in Blois, attributed to the Bolognese artist Lavinia Fontana and dated around 1595, may be that very portrait. The artist, who was on good terms with both the celebrated naturalist and with the senator Mario Casali, probably painted the portrait during the stay of the marchesa and the girl in April 1594 in Casali's house in Bologna, where Aldrovandi was able to examine the girl's physical appearance. Whatever Aldrovandi's personal motives may have been for placing this portrait here, it serves to evoke his medical skill as a physician, even though he only practised as one professionally on a very occasional basis, as when he wrote a short treatise on vertigo for Paolo Ghiselli, the private secretary of the Bolognese pope, who suffered from it.[62]

Aldrovandi's suburban villa was no cosy rural cottage, but neither was it a retreat for study; indeed, in his exchange with Cardinal Gabriele Paleotti, he wrote that, as he was in his villa, he had very few books at his disposal.[63] It afforded a relaxed atmosphere in which to receive – and impress – a visitor like Melchior de Villagómez, a Spaniard who had travelled in Peru and who visited Aldrovandi in his country villa in 1587.[64] It also conveyed the message of the leisure (*otium*) – that is, freedom from the constraints of business or other activities (*negotium*) – accorded to a gentleman. Besides the five rooms to be shown to visitors, there must also have been private quarters, utilities and an enclosure for animals (perhaps the place where Aldrovandi kept the drunken monkey mentioned by Lorenzo Giacomini in a letter of 1592).[65] So the combination of a portrait gallery, a room decorated with scenes from Homeric epic, and three more filled with moralizing emblems is an iconographic programme that emulates those implemented in princely courts like the one in the *studiolo* of Francesco de' Medici from some fifteen years

64 Lavinia Fontana (attrib.), *Antonietta González*, c. 1594–5, oil on canvas.

earlier. In those, the programme would generally allude to the particular qualities of the ruler (military prowess, wisdom, piety and so on) and often play on the name of that ruler. Aldrovandi played the same game here, exploiting the resonances of his name to the full and displaying that resourcefulness embodied in the stock epithet *polytropos* ('wily' or 'resourceful') of the hero of the *Odyssey*.

SEVEN

Ornithologia and After: The Collection and the Posthumous Publications

he Swiss naturalist Conrad Gessner was fortunate enough to witness the publication of almost all of his voluminous works on natural history and philology before his death from the plague at the age of 49 in 1565. No such good fortune was granted to Aldrovandi, although he lived to the ripe old age of 82. Besides his youthful publication on Roman collections of antiquities from 1556 and a pharmaceutical manual in 1574, only the three volumes on birds and one on insects saw the light of day before his death on 4 May 1605.

Publication of the three volumes on ornithology commenced in 1599, but it is evident in a letter from Calzolari to Aldrovandi in September 1554 (only a few months after they had scaled Monte Baldo together) asking him for his opinion on a *Passer troglodites* (a wren) that Aldrovandi's interest in birds was lifelong.[1] Given his desire to obtain eyewitness evidence where possible, the field of ornithology offered him more scope to observe species in their habitat than, say, elephants or whales would have done.

Thanks to Laurent Pinon's painstaking study of the making of the *Ornithologia*, we can gain insight into Aldrovandi's method of working on a publication from its first conception in manuscript form in 1587 down to the printing stage ten years later.[2] Planned as a work that would supersede the already vast compilation by Gessner, it nevertheless largely followed the same method dear to the humanists of amassing passages from the

writings of all previous authors on the species in question. The
existence of two kinds of lists among the preparatory papers for
the *Ornithologia* makes this explicit: lists of the authorities cited
by Gessner, and lists of those consulted by Aldrovandi who are
not mentioned by Gessner. This consultation was a team effort,
as Aldrovandi depended on a number of assistants. It was their
task to go through the volumes in his library excerpting passages
bearing on the species in question and indicating page number
and shelf reference. The variety in the handwriting of these passages reflects the labour of many hands. A six-hundred-page
manuscript of a Latin translation of Pierre Belon's *Histoire de la
nature des oyseaux*, on the other hand, is entirely in Aldrovandi's own
handwriting; he must have made the translation to facilitate his
task later on. It cannot have been easy for him: in a letter to Clusius
from 1590, he confessed that his grasp of French was rather
approximate.[3] In the same letter he asked Clusius to send him an
image and description of any 'exotic' bird that might come his way
– an indication that there was still room to insert additional items
in the projected volumes. By the spring of the following year, the
catalogue of bird images contained more than seven hundred
items, but Aldrovandi felt there was little point in sending it to
Clusius because the vernacular names of so many exotic birds
would be of little use without the visual images and verbal
descriptions.[4]

The extracts appeared in the chronological order in which
each publication had been consulted in turn. They were then cut
up into separate items and pasted together on large sheets in
alphabetical order to provide a synoptic view of all of the available information concerning that species, or concerning birds
in general. On the basis of these, Aldrovandi covered no fewer
than 6,000 manuscript pages with the Latin text of a preliminary
version of the work, divided into *Ornithologia generalis* and *Ornithologia
specialis*. Besides drawing on the more recent work of Belon and

on the voluminous accounts of the writers of antiquity, Aldrovandi
added new information based on his own first-hand investiga-
tions, although 'the direct, personal observations are diluted in
the ocean of citations; suffocated by the past, they often lose their
original liveliness.'[5] An example is provided by the anatomical
dissections that he carried out in the winter of 1588. The preparation of designs of these enabled him to dispense with a number of
lengthy descriptions in the published work, substituting detailed
printed images in their place. This is an indication of his close
supervision of the process of combining text and image on the
printed page. Indeed, his insistence on remaining in control, even
when his sight and health were failing, led him to demand that
the printer of the work, Francesco de' Franceschi in Venice,
transfer his equipment to Bologna and instal it next to Aldrovandi's
own home. When he grew dissatisfied with the rate at which de'
Franceschi was working, Aldrovandi persisted in making this a
condition of the appointment of a successor.

   A further important element in the publication was the large
number of indices, proudly listing the various names of birds in
seventeen different languages. The addition of twenty pages on
the use of the eagle in heraldry gave him an opportunity to mention
by name a large number of noble families, who would duly appear
in the indices as well – a ploy that we can regard as a further
symptom of his pressing desire and need to secure the patronage
of the powerful and influential. Although in 1566 Aldrovandi
had been given special dispensation (which was extended to
Uterwer in 1611) to own a copy of the work of Gessner, the Swiss
Protestant naturalist's books had been placed on the index of
censored works by the authorities in Rome with whom Aldrovandi
had already had a brush in the past – it was still necessary to
obtain the permission of the Congregation of the Inquisition to
reprint one of Aldrovandi's own works as late as 1658[6] – so he
must have felt it more prudent to refer to him by the vague

designation 'German' or 'Ornithologus'. We may suspect that the same person lies behind Cassiano dal Pozzo's references to 'esteemed German authors'.[7]

The images printed in the volumes were also the result of a collaborative effort. Aldrovandi claimed to have employed four painters in his house for almost forty years, in which time they had made some 7,000 images of 'animals, plants and fossils'.[8] There were two further stages before printing could begin: namely, the copying of the original to the woodblock and the cutting of the woodblock ready for printing. Clearly, deviations from the original could occur in each of these two stages; while Aldrovandi could give instructions to check the faithfulness of the artist's work with regard to colour and other aspects, it was much harder for him to intervene in the execution of either of the latter activities.

That he was actively involved in the composition of each of the three volumes of the work before it finally went to press is revealed in a letter from 1602. In February of that year he wrote to the erudite teenage scholar Nicolas-Claude Fabri de Peiresc that, although he experienced great difficulty in finding a suitable artist during Carnival, he was nevertheless able to send him an image of a flamingo that was created while the festival was on, 'which will be printed in the third volume of the composition of my *Ornithologia*'.[9] Like his correspondent Charles de l'Écluse, whose desire to incorporate the latest stop press items resulted in a 21-page appendix to the 1605 edition of his *Exoticorum libri decem*, Aldrovandi was keeping the door open for new arrivals as long as he could.[10] That volume of the *Ornithologia* was published in 1603, by which time the ageing naturalist was bedridden and had decided to make his last will and testament. Two years later he was dead.

IN LEAVING HIS ENTIRE collection to the Senate of Bologna
in his last will and testament, Ulisse Aldrovandi stipulated that
nothing was to be neglected, ceded or taken outside the city. This
is not what happened in the end. At first the collection was formally
installed in the quarters of the civic head of government (*gonfalo-
niere*) in the Palazzo Pubblico in 1617, and forty years later the
Aldrovandi collection was joined by the (much smaller) museum
of Ferdinando Cospi, which included the Codex Cospi, a valuable
document of ritual from the Mixtec-Puebla area of Mexico that
was probably brought to Bologna by a Spanish Dominican friar
in 1532–3. The manuscript inventories of the two collections
show that they were kept physically separate.[11] In 1742, however,
the Aldrovandi collection was split: the books, including the paintings of *naturalia* that served as the basis for woodcuts, passed into
what is now Bologna University Library, while the larger part of
its contents was transferred from the Palazzo Pubblico to Palazzo
Poggi as part of the Institute of Science created by Luigi Ferdinando
Marsili in 1711. Aldrovandi had employed a specialist block-cutter
from Nuremberg, Cristoforo Coriolano, for almost a decade to
produce the woodblocks for his publications, and successive inventories indicate that they must have numbered more than 5,000.[12]

The individual items were divided thematically between six
different exhibition rooms. With the passing of time and changes
in tastes, the integrity of the collection suffered. Some items fell
into disrepair or went missing: for example, some of Aldrovandi's
'curiosities' of natural history may have been among those removed
by Napoleon's commissioners in 1797.[13] Each move had the poten-
tial to transform how the items were presented and interpreted.
Those from the room of antiquities were moved to the university
museum of antiquities in 1803. Later in the same century the
collection of this museum was merged with the Museo Civico
Archeologico, created to display the prehistory of Bologna, while
some items deemed unsuited to that purpose found their way to

what was then the Museo Luigi Pigorini (now the Museo delle Civiltà in Rome) in the capital.

ONE OF THE CONDITIONS of Aldrovandi's legacy was that work on publishing should go ahead. For that purpose he entrusted the supervision of the task to a custodian who was to work from a room in the museum. *De reliquis animalibus exanguibus*, a work on bloodless creatures (a term which, since Aristotle, has covered cephalopods, crustaceans and a number of other animals that are categorized differently today), edited by Aldrovandi's Flemish assistant Johann Cornelius Uterwer, appeared in Bologna in 1606 and was the first of the numerous posthumous publications. They continued to appear, down to a work on trees published in 1668. Uterwer, who succeeded Aldrovandi as professor of natural history and was appointed as the first custodian of Aldrovandi's library and collection, must have worked closely with Aldrovandi on preparing the book on bloodless creatures for publication before the latter's death. That posthumous publication may therefore be supposed to represent as faithfully as possible the views of the Bolognese naturalist. By the 1630s and '40s, however, the hand of Aldrovandi in the publications was less dominant. It had not disappeared entirely, for 366 of the woodcuts for the posthumous publication on monsters had already been prepared by 1602 – in other words, under his supervision.[14] All the same, the intervention of Bartolomeo Ambrosini, custodian of the Aldrovandi museum from 1632 to 1657, in the preparation of this work for publication in 1642, as well as the slightly earlier publications on viviparous and oviparous quadrupeds (1637) and serpents and dragons (1640), makes it more difficult to consider these publications as direct reflections of Aldrovandi's own thought, however closely they may have approximated to it. As for the last of these posthumous publications, the *Dendrología*, its editor,

65 Caterpillars, dragonfly and monkey, dated 1630, from Aldrovandi, *Tavole*, Biblioteca Universitaria Bologna.

Ovidio Montalbani, used only a small part of Aldrovandi's original material, ignoring his herbarium and his painted drawings, and selecting only those aspects that were monstrous or anomalous in some way in accordance with the change in taste that had taken place in the intervening 62 years since Aldrovandi's death.[15]

The collection of painted drawings also continued to expand after Aldrovandi's death. A miscellaneous album containing 87 painted images of birds, plants, reptiles, insects and more includes individual items dated in the second decade of the seventeenth century (illus. 65),[16] and the presence of several images pasted on to a single page to form a collage is more reminiscent of the work of Hoefnagel than of Aldrovandi himself. The signature on some of them points to Antonio Cerva, the Bolognese minia-turist employed in the decoration of Aldrovandi's villa. It may be presumed that he had access to Aldrovandi's images, and indeed some of his versions, like his painted image of a bat, are derived from the published ornithological volumes. Aldrovandi donated a hand-coloured copy of the first volume of this work – one of the 25 copies that he had printed on de luxe paper – to the library of the Bolognese Senate, which was open to the public.[17] Cerva probably intended this collection of images for private use, in order to furnish him with models during his later career. Other collections of painted drawings of animals in various places (such as Bologna, Rome, London and Suffolk) and of varying quality show that both the Aldrovandian collection of painted draw-ings and the Aldrovandian publications continued to be used as models to be copied.[18] The *Musaeum metallicum* was prepared for posthumous publication by Ambrosini with editorial and promotional assistance from the Portuguese bibliophile Vicente Nogueira.[19] It has been suggested that a drawing of a piece of coral in the paper museum of Cassiano dal Pozzo, which is unusual in that it is monochrome and on the reverse bears captions to the items illustrated on the recto, may be an original drawing of specimens in Aldrovandi's museum by one of his assistants. The name of the German artist-engraver Cornelius Schwindt from Frankfurt am Main, who may have been recruited for Aldrovandi in Florence by Francesco de' Medici, has been suggested as a possible candidate.[20]

Peter Paul Rubens bought a copy of the *Ornithologia* in 1613, and went on to purchase the zoological works for use in his pictures involving animals.[21] However, by the mid-seventeenth century attitudes had shifted, and what had been presented as a collection of objects with an encyclopaedic scope by Aldrovandi became assimilated to the spirit of a baroque theatre of marvels and portents. It is symptomatic that the 1667 publication on trees was edited by Montalbani, who was much closer to the baroque sensibility of Athanasius Kircher than to Aldrovandi's more natural-scientific approach.[22]

RECEPTION

We have already seen how eager Ferdinando de' Medici was to obtain each of the three volumes of the *Ornithologia* as soon as they appeared. Joachim Camerarius the Younger, who had studied medicine in Germany before completing his studies in Bologna and Padua, was the author of an emblem book on birds and insects published in 1596 that drew mainly on emblem books dating from much earlier, but he also attempted to update his information where possible. Commenting on the 54th emblem in that book, depicting shearwaters from one of the Italian Tremiti islands, he wrote: 'An accurate description of this bird was sent to me by Mr Ulisse Aldrovandi, Professor in Bologna, most expert in natural history, whose most perfect books on birds and other things, which he is preparing for publication, are eagerly awaited.'[23] He was thus another reader who was excited by the imminent publication of the three volumes on birds by Aldrovandi, with whom he had been corresponding for some time. Indeed, in the following year Aldrovandi begged Camerarius to send anything new that had come his way to enrich his own museum.[24]

Two years later, the errant and erratic young Dutch physician Johannes van Heeck, who was employed in the Orsini castle in Scandriglia to the northeast of Rome, wrote two letters to Aldrovandi in which, besides fulsomely contrasting his own meagre knowledge as a student (*discípulus*) of natural science with the omniscience of his addressee, he fulminated against the use of foreign plants and minerals in the preparation of medicinal remedies. Likening the current medical situation to the familiar rhetorical figure of the ship of fools, he accused its practitioners of turning their back on local remedies and using 'foreign plants and falsified drugs to combine Asia, Africa, Europe and the New World in a single prescription'. His tirade culminated in a plea to Aldrovandi to 'lay the foundations of a new medicine'.[25] Whether or not the word *discipulus* should be taken to imply that Aldrovandi could be regarded as a master, it is evident from the tone of the letter that van Heeck held the Bolognese scientist in high regard.

In 1603 the Dutch physician joined the Roman nobleman Federico Cesi and two of his associates to form the Lincean Academy in Rome. Two years before Aldrovandi's death, this new scientific creation – which was disbanded at the end of 1604 but reconstituted in 1610 – was dedicated to the kind of scientific experiment for which its best-known member, Galileo Galilei, was to become famous, together with researches of a more arcane kind, all aimed at a renewal of the stultified education provided by the universities. Like Aldrovandi, the Linceans were fascinated by the prospect of new scientific discoveries opened up by the results of the botanical expedition of Francisco Hernández in the New World in the 1570s. However, the Bolognese scientist's attempts to gain more information from the Naples-based Linceans Fabio Colonna and Giovanni Battista della Porta about

the American materials that had been brought to the city in 1589
by Nardo Antonio Recchi met with evasive or negative responses.
Federico Cesi, on the other hand, was able to acquire Recchi's
text in 1610 and immediately conceived the idea of the publication
of an ambitious work on the natural history of the Americas.[26]

The slow but steady maturation of the Lincean project grad-
ually eclipsed the importance of Aldrovandi as a point of reference. The Lincean Cassiano dal Pozzo, showing more reticence
than Aldrovandi had ever done, published an *Uccelliera* in 1622
under the name of Giovanni Pietro Olina.[27] In this work he took
Aldrovandi's *Ornithologia* as a point of reference, but he did not
do so uncritically. For example, on the cirl bunting (*zivolo*), Cassiano
noted that Aldrovandi had written that in Bologna the bird was
called a *raparino*, but commented that in Tuscany this name referred
to a different bird. Above all, the quality engravings by Antonio
Tempesta or Vincenzo Leonardi, many of them showing the birds
life size, are of a more consistently high level than those of any
predecessor. For example, the engraving illustrating how to make
food for nightingales is full of lively details: as well as illustrating
the various stages in the preparation of the mixture, it shows two
lutes hanging on the wall, a cat and a dog, and two birds in cages
(illus. 66).[28] Cassiano's ornithological researches did not stop in
1622. He went on to write several treatises on birds, including one
on the pelican, and corresponded at length with Peiresc on the
flamingo.[29]

By the end of 1628, Colonna wrote to Cesi that he had seen
Aldrovandi's 1606 (posthumous) publication *De reliquis animalibus exanguibus, nempe de mollibus, crustaceis, testaceis et zoophytis*, but he
complained that such a work deserved better woodcuts, especially
in the section on the Testacea, which were not only crudely represented, but in most cases shown the wrong way round as well.
They compared unfavourably with the woodcuts in the *Exoticorum
libri decem* of Charles de l'Écluse published a year earlier than the

Aldrovandian work.[30] When a North African oryx dispatched by
Peiresc to Cardinal Francesco Barberini arrived in Rome in 1634,
it offered image collectors like Cassiano the opportunity to obtain
more faithful copies of unfamiliar exotic animals. Aldrovandi
had included a woodcut of such an animal, an 'ox with twisted
horns' (*Bos strepticeros*, illus. 67), in his work on cloven-hoofed
quadrupeds (QBH, pp. 368–9). Cassiano's verdict on the quality

66 'How to Cook Food for Nightingales', supplementary engraving
for Giovanni Pietro Olina, *Uccelliera overo discorso della natura e proprieta di
diversi uccelli . . .* (1622).

of this image, which Aldrovandi had received from the court of Rudolph II, was dismissive:

> In his work on cloven-hoofed quadrupeds, where he talks about the Bos Strepticeros, Aldrovandi inserts a figure that is so terrible and clumsy that it is impossible to tell what animal it is, nor does he say which country it comes from, nor anything else except that he had received a beautiful image of that exotic and rare animal.[31]

Concerns about the availability of engravers and the quality of printed images, which were to dog the Lincean *Mexican Thesaurus* project as well, were coming increasingly to the fore. In 1610 Francesco, the son of Ferrante Imperato, complained to the Lincean Johannes Faber about the lack of quality draughtsmen

67 Ox with twisted horns, from Aldrovandi, *Quadrupedum omnium bisulcorum historia* (1621).

and engravers in Naples to engrave the fossils in the family collection (the Neapolitan engraver Giovan Andrea Magliulo was probably dead by this date).[32] In Rome, both Johannes Faber and Federico Cesi were well aware of the shortcomings of the technique of woodcut illustration, and they regretted the obstacles, particularly of an economic kind, which barred them access to the higher quality of printmakers on the other side of the Alps.[33] They had in mind the superior quality of the copperplate images published in 1613 in the *Hortus Eystettensis*, a compendium of the plants contained in the episcopal garden of Eichstätt, thanks to the patronage of Bishop Konrad von Gemmingen. In Rome, it is true, the *Aquatilium animalium historiae* of Ippolito Salviani had been printed in 1557–8 with 98 copper engravings, and was marketed in a standard edition sold at 35 giulii and a de luxe hand-coloured edition at 70 giulii, but then as Salviani was the physician to three successive popes as well as a university professor at the Sapienza, he could count on the generous financial support of the Vatican librarian Cardinal Marcello Cervini.[34] The cost of having copperplate engravings made of the quantity of images envisaged for the *Mexican Thesaurus* or Aldrovandi's voluminous works would have been exorbitant.

Such considerations of quality did not deter several writers later in the century from recycling Aldrovandian woodcuts even though they were growing increasingly out of date. Juan Eusebio Nieremberg copied Aldrovandi's bird of paradise in his *Historia naturae* of 1635, and Athanasius Kircher copied such Aldrovandian images as the fossil *Vomeropsis* fish and, in a stylized version, the anthropomorphic marble image of a hermit in his *Mundus subterraneus* of 1664 (MM, pp. 453 and 755).[35] Though both writers were Jesuits with a particular axe to grind, the baroque science of Nieremberg, even though he had access to the original Hernández material, was largely confined to the bookish culture of Madrid, while the more exuberant Kircher at the head of one of the most famous museums in Europe envisaged a work whose spectacular mediatic impact was designed to impress the outside world.[36]

Another emulator of the encyclopaedic sweep of Aldrovandi's works is the Calvinist Johann Jonston, born in Poland to a Scottish father and a German mother in 1603. The six volumes of his *Historiae naturalis* were first published in Frankfurt am Main between 1649 and 1653.[37] The images of 569 birds that feature on the 62 plates of his *Historiae naturalis de avibus* of 1650 are pillaged from Gessner, Aldrovandi and others down to the recent publication of the birds of Brazil by Georg Marcgraf, but they differ from Aldrovandi's publication in two important ways: they are high-quality copper engravings, and they are classified in only two groups – land birds and water birds – arranged synoptically in series on a single page. This device relied on the strength of the visual presentation to bring out the relations between the different varieties shown together and was intended to delight as much as to edify. Among the plates in his *Historia naturalis de quadrupedibus* (1652), Jonston continued his borrowings from Aldrovandi. Plate 58 copies the Aldrovandian image of an exotic wether (illus. 68), a ram without horns, with a white body and a black head and hooves. Aldrovandi had not seen the animal himself but his nephew in Rome, Giuliano Griffoni, had communicated the image to him. The maker of the image appears to have drawn on a marble sculpture of the animal, perhaps from the second century AD, to be found in Cardinal Ferdinando de' Medici's collection of sculptures of animals in the Villa Medici, Rome.[38]

That image has an afterlife: the Latin inscription on the tree trunk supporting the body of the sheep, restored and recomposed in the eighteenth century using parts of the original sculpture but incorrectly substituting a white head, now in the Animal Room of the Vatican Museums, gives its name as VERVEX ÆTHIOPICUS and refers to the plate from Jonston's publication. Whoever

was responsible for the learned inscription was evidently more familiar with the later image than with that by Aldrovandi's illustrator.

This eclipsing of Aldrovandi's natural history by that of his seventeenth-century successors is an indicator of a major shift. The humanist dream of compiling information about everything under the sun, culled from everything that had ever been written about it and enriched with some contemporary observations, had run up against its ineluctable limit. There was simply a point beyond which the exponential amassing of information about the natural world became unmanageable. In summing up the fortune and significance of Aldrovandi, Sandra Tugnoli Pattaro characterized him as a Janus-like figure: facing backwards to the encyclopaedic erudition of Aristotle and those who followed in his tradition, and forwards to the scientific observation practised

68 *Vervex aethiopicus* (black-headed ram), from Aldrovandi, *Quadrupedum omnium bisulcorum historia* (1621).

by the Linceans, most famously Galileo Galilei.[39] Similarly, Giuseppe Olmi referred to 'a double track in continuous tension between rationality and fantasy'.[40]

The printed works of Aldrovandi, in which 'he was primarily concerned with his own external image and felt the need to say everything about everything, to unload centuries of studies and interpretations on the reader' are unreadable as such.[41] They are reference works, as the copious indices indicate, produced with the aim of providing an encyclopaedic archive of material but not for delectation. They had been overtaken by the growth of specialist publications: the Lincean *Mexican Treasury* on animals and plants of the New World that incorporated the latest information about American animals brought to Rome by Dominican friars in 1625; the work of Georg Marcgraf on the natural history of Brazil, first published in 1648; or Maria Sibylla Merian's book on the insects of Surinam in 1705.

Scientists continued to refer to Aldrovandi's classifications. Commenting on 'as for the stork, the fir trees are her house' from Psalm 104, the polymath Thomas Browne discussed Aldrovandi's pages on the nesting habits of storks with characteristic wit, suggesting that this may have been the case in biblical times before the construction of houses with chimneys. And in the same publication he referred explicitly to the catalogues of the collections of Aldrovandi, Calzolari and others before proceeding to present his own catalogue of the fictitious *Musaeum Clausum* containing 'some remarkable Books, Antiquities, Pictures and Rarities of several kinds, scarce or never seen by any man now living'.[42] More prosaically, among the manuscript catalogues of the early collections of the Ashmolean Museum in Oxford, the book of the Principal of Brasenose in the Vice-Chancellor's Consolidated Catalogue of 1695 is evidence that the compiler, Edward Lhwyd of Jesus College, was still drawing on Aldrovandi and Belon as well as on the later works of Jonston, Marcgraf and others, such

as the flying fish *mílvus*, the sucking fish or *remora*, toucan beaks
or the black-backed gull.[43] In the 1730s, the Spanish physician
Fernández Navarrete, author of a *Historia natural de España*, continued to refer to Aldrovandi in connection with petrified stones
and his labelling of figured stones as *Marmor anthropomorphon*.[44]
When Carl Linnaeus arrived as a first-year student in Lund in
1727, one of the first authors he read was Ulisse Aldrovandi.[45] And
when Sir Hans Sloane acquired a portrait in oils of a gentleman
improbably inscribed VLISSES ALDROVANDI, he must have wished
that it was a true likeness of the Bolognese physician and naturalist. With his collection of 18,000 items, Aldrovandi could be
considered a spiritual ancestor of Sloane's own personality as a
physician and naturalist with a collection arranged along similar
lines but amounting to more than 40,000 natural-historical and
mineral items alone by the time it was bequeathed to the British
Museum in 1753.[46]

AS WE SAW IN THE OPENING chapter, in spite of the fact that
Aldrovandi's first publication was on the antiquities in Roman
gardens, it was not followed up by any others on the subject,
and there is little evidence of a serious or sustained antiquarian
interest on his part. Comparisons with such figures as Cassiano
dal Pozzo or Nicolas-Claude Fabri de Peiresc serve to highlight
the difference. A visitor to Cassiano's residence in Rome would
have been struck by the antiquities and inscriptions inserted
into the walls of the courtyard, the casts of the reliefs on Trajan's
Column and the many ancient statues, before perusing the paper
museum of drawings of every aspect of ancient life from religion
to architecture. According to his biographer Carlo Dati, the paper
museum was contained in 23 volumes, though the dispersal of
the collection after Cassiano's death makes it very difficult to
quantify the exact number of drawings.

As for Peiresc, it is enough to cite the rich correspondence that he exchanged with Lelio Pasqualini after their meeting in 1600. Peiresc's admiration for the elderly numismatic expert emerges clearly from a letter he sent to William Camden in 1608, in which he called Pasqualini 'easily the leading one among the experts on antiquity in Italy'.[47] The Bolognese Pasqualini was made a canon of the Basilica of Santa Maria Maggiore in Rome at the election of the Bolognese Pope Gregory XIII in 1572, and devoted himself to collecting ancient and early Christian coins, intaglios and gems when church duties permitted. Peiresc's detailed comments on a number of these show that the epistolary contact with Pasqualini played a formative part in building up the young French scholar's expertise in the field. It is well known that neither Pasqualini nor Peiresc could be induced to publish their findings, though they did write manuscript treatises; what they enjoyed was conversation with like-minded members of the République des Lettres. Peiresc's well-stocked library contained all the major publications on Roman antiquities from Vitruvius and Serlio to Flavio Biondo and Pirro Ligorio,[48] yet a search in the database containing the catalogues of the major French libraries apart from the Bibliothèque nationale between 1556 and 1700 has revealed that none of them possessed Aldrovandi's 1556 publication on the antiquities of Rome. Peiresc had eight volumes of Aldrovandi's works, but not *Le antichità della città di Roma*.[49] Nor is Aldrovandi's list of antiquities in Rome mentioned among the sources referred to in an authoritative 1993 survey of the place of Cassiano in the tradition of drawing from the antique.[50]

If we turn to consider the other publications by Aldrovandi, it is hard to resist the conclusion that his timing was flawed. His contact with Guillaume Rondelet on the fish market in Rome may well have stimulated his interest in studying fishes and other elements of the natural world, but while the illustrated works on ichthyology by Rondelet, Pierre Belon, Ippolito Salviani and Conrad Gessner all appeared in the decade of the 1550s, Aldrovandi's *De piscibus* was not published until more than half a century later, seven years after its author's death.[51] And, as we have seen, the publication dates of his other works follow the same pattern. By the time of the publication of the second part of *Don Quixote* in 1615, terms such as 'troglodytes' and 'anthropophagi' had lost any specific meaning, becoming instead just simple terms of abuse.[52] Indeed, many of the woodcut images in the *Monstrorum historia* published in 1642 were already at least a century old, and the inconsistencies in the application of the term 'monster' to a variety of human, animal and celestial phenomena were due to the influence of the views of Fortunio Liceti, published in Padua in 1616 in his *De monstrorum caussis, natura et differentiis libri duo*, on Aldrovandi's posthumous editor Ambrosini.[53] Like the father of Tristram Shandy, falling more and more behind in the composition of his *Tristrapaedia* to meet the needs of his growing son, Aldrovandi's drive to accumulate more and more rendered him increasingly out of step with the times. By the middle of the eighteenth century, Buffon – an author hardly noted for Beckettian terseness – could pass a very negative verdict on Aldrovandi as a scientist:

> After sixty years of work, Aldrovandi, the most hardworking and knowledgeable of all the naturalists, has left immense volumes on natural history that have been successively printed, most of them after his death: they could be reduced to a tenth part if you were to remove all the things that are useless and extraneous to his subject, to this prolixity which, I declare, is exhausting.[54]

Even when we make allowances for the tunnel vision that judges its predecessors by its own later achievements, Buffon's judgement called into question the piling up of sections on 'Names,

Habits, Voice, Food, and Anatomy, Antipathies and Sympathies, Physiognomy, Epithets, Emblems and Symbols, Fables, Hieroglyphics, Proverbs, Allegories, Morals, Omens, and Symbolic Images, to name just some of the headings' that no longer had, or has, a place in scientific thought.[55] A case in point is Aldrovandi's entry on the horse: against four pages of scientific zoology, there are 290 containing all the other extraneous snippets of information.[56] As Michel Foucault summed it up:

> One and a single form of knowledge is required to bring together all that has been *seen* and *known*, all that has been told, by nature and by people, by the language of the world, traditions and poets . . . The great tripartition, so simple in appearance and so immediate, of Observation, Document and Fable did not exist.[57]

By the end of the nineteenth century, the tide had definitively turned against this notion of science. Writing on the entry of the fossil collections of Pedro Scalabrini to the museum of Entre Ríos, Argentina, in 1884, the Italo-Argentinean palaeontologist Florentino Ameghino wrote: 'The time is past in which these were a simple luxury object and curiosity where people went to amuse themselves at the sight of two-headed monsters, or stones that with a dose of good will represented what they chose to see in them.'[58] Still, it is the thirst for accumulation that gives Ulisse Aldrovandi a special place among Renaissance collectors of *naturalia*. The first step towards the creation of a collection seems to have been the filling of two volumes of his herbarium with the fruits of his first botanizing expedition in 1551. As the radius of his own movements began to shrink, he increasingly came to rely on a widespread network of friends, fellow naturalists, patrons and others in Italy and abroad to supply him with objects and/ or images for his collection. Towards the end of his life, the 18,000 varieties of natural specimens and the 7,000 dried plants in fifteen volumes, supplemented by seventeen volumes of images of animals, plants, minerals and monsters, all amounted to what was a *scientific* collection. Though it is sometimes hard to draw a clear-cut boundary, it was essentially conceived as something different from and more functional than the collections of curiosities to be found in the Kunst- und Wunderkammern that were springing up in the courts of Europe at the time.[59] And it was undoubtedly the largest in Europe, attracting visitors in droves.

In the end, it was to Aldrovandi's great merit that he took the initiative to create a scientific collection on such a scale and bequeathed it to the Bolognese Senate to ensure that it would be of public benefit. But above all, he recognized the skills and knowledge to be found among not only fellow academics in the towns and cities, but those who tested substances in their dispensaries or went out to botanize in the fields and the mountains, inspect fish on the local markets, or search for fossils and other minerals on or beneath the surface of the earth. They were all linked through their common interests in a collective enterprise built up through a system of exchanges in which the gift of an item would be made in the hope of securing a gift or favour in return, or a mention in the museum or publications of the recipient. That collective enterprise is what lies concealed behind the name of the Renaissance humanist Ulisse Aldrovandi.

CHRONOLOGY

This biographical outline is based on Giuseppe Montalenti, 'Aldrovandi, Ulisse', in *Dizionario biografico degli Italiani*, vol. 11 (Rome, 1960), pp. 118–24, and Sandra Tugnoli Pattaro, 'Nota biografica', in *Natura picta: Ulisse Aldrovandi*, ed. Alessandro Alessandrini and Alessandro Ceregato (Bologna, 2007), pp. 612–19.

1522   Born in Bologna on 11 September
1529   Death of his father
1538   Travels through France to Spain
1539   Commences study of jurisprudence at the University
        of Bologna
1547–8 Studies logic, philosophy and medicine in Bologna
        and Padua
1549   Arrested and imprisoned in Rome on charges of heresy
1550   Released in Rome and develops interest in ichthyology
        and botany there
1553   Graduates from the University of Bologna in philosophy
        and medicine
1554   Ascent of Monte Baldo with Luca Ghini, Francesco
        Calzolari and others to botanize there; begins to teach
        philosophy in Bologna
1556   Begins to teach medical botany; publication of his
        Delle statue antiche in Venice
1559   Promotion to the chair of *filosofia ordinaria*
1560   Birth of an illegitimate son, Achille; assigned to teach
        about fossils, plants and animals
1561   Inaugurates the first chair of natural history in Bologna,
        which he holds until 1600
1563   Marries Paola Macchiavelli
1564   Conducts anatomical dissections
1565   Death of Paola on 5 April; marries Francesca Fontana
        on 10 October
1568   Appointed director of the new public botanical garden
        in Bologna

1574	Publishes the first Bolognese *Antidotario*, a pharmaceutical manual
1575	Outbreak of the theriac controversy
1577	Death of his son Achille; first visit to see the collection in Florence of Francesco de' Medici, Grand Duke of Tuscany
1594	Invites Francesco de' Franceschi to come to Bologna to print the works of natural history that are the result of his researches
1599	Publication of the first of three volumes on ornithology
1605	Dies 4 May and buried in the church of Santo Stefano in Bologna

REFERENCES

Preface

1 Julius von Schlosser, *Kunst- und Wunderkammern der Spätrenaissance*, 2nd edn (Braunschweig, 1978), p. 204; Giuseppe Olmi, 'Science-Honour-Metaphor: Italian Cabinets of the Sixteenth and Seventeenth Centuries', and Laura Laurencich-Minelli, 'Museography and Ethnographical Collections in Bologna during the Sixteenth and Seventeenth Centuries', in *The Origins of Museums*, ed. Oliver Impey and Arthur MacGregor (Oxford, 1985), pp. 5–16 and 17–23 respectively.

2 Alessandro Tosi, *Ulisse Aldrovandi e la Toscana: carteggio e testimonianze documentarie* (Florence, 1989), p. 23.

3 Ibid., p. 190.

4 Alessandro Tosi, *Portraits of Men and Ideas: Images of Science in Italy from the Renaissance to the Nineteenth Century* (Pisa, 2007).

5 Dario Franchini et al., eds, *La scienza a corte: collezionismo eclettico, natura e immagine a Mantova fra Rinascimento e manierismo* (Rome, 1979).

6 Giuseppe Olmi, *L'inventario del mondo: catalogazione della natura e luoghi del sapere nella prima età moderna* (Bologna, 1992), p. 38 n. 57.

7 Giuseppe Olmi, 'Bologna nel secolo XVI: Una capitale europea della ricerca naturalistica', in *Crocevia e capitale della migrazione artistica: forestieri a Bologna e bolognese nel mondo (secoli XV–XVI)*, ed. Sabine Frommel (Bologna, 2010), pp. 61–80.

8 Dante, *Inferno*, XVI.137; Mary Watt, 'Dante and the New World', in *The New World in Early Modern Italy, 1492–1750*, ed. Elizabeth Horodowich and Lia Markey (Cambridge, 2017), pp. 34–46.

Prologue: Housing and Displaying a Collection

1 Laura Laurencich-Minelli, 'Museography and Ethnographical Collections in Bologna during the Sixteenth and Seventeenth

Centuries', in *The Origins of Museums*, ed. Oliver Impey and Arthur MacGregor (Oxford, 1985), pp. 17–23; Giuseppe Olmi, *L'inventario del mondo: catalogazione della natura e luoghi del sapere nella prima età moderna* (Bologna, 1992), p. 281.

2 Olmi, *L'inventario del mondo*, p. 53.

3 Jacopo Antonio Buoni, *Del terremoto* (Modena, 1571), p. 45, cited in Eugenio Battisti, *L'antirinascimento*, 2nd edn (Turin, 2005), pp. 346–7.

4 See also Olmi, *L'inventario del mondo*, p. 107 and n. 289.

5 Florike Egmond and Peter Mason, *The Mammoth and the Mouse: Microhistory and Morphology* (Baltimore, MD, and London, 1997), pp. 7–18.

6 Alessandro Tosi, *Ulisse Aldrovandi e la Toscana: carteggio e testimonianze documentarie* (Florence, 1989), pp. 431–2; Paolo Bertelli, *La vergine e il drago: Lo strano caso dei coccodrilli nei santuari mariani* (Mantua, 2018).

7 Giuseppe Olmi and Lucia Tongiorgi Tomasi, *De piscibus: La bottega artistica di Ulisse Aldrovandi e l'immagine naturalistica* (Rome, 1993), p. 25. The classic study of casting small creatures from life is still Ernst Kris, 'Der Stil "rustique". Die Verwendung des Naturabgusses bei Wenzel Jamnitzer und Bernard Palissy', *Jahrbuch der kunsthistorichen Sammlungen in Wien*, I (1926), pp. 137–208.

8 Borgarutio Borgarucci, 'To the Readers', preface inserted before Part Two of *Delle cose che si portano dall'Indie Occidentali pertinenti all'vso della medicina: Raccolte, & trattate dal Dottor Nicolò Monardes, Medico di Siuiglia* (Venice, 1589).

9 Mario Cermenati, 'Francesco Calzolari e le sue lettere all'Aldrovandi', *Annali di Botanica*, VII/1 (1908), p. 125.

10 Calzolari to Joachim Camerarius II, 3 September 1583, in Giuseppe Olmi, 'Per la storia dei rapporti scientifici fra Italia e Germania: le lettere di Francesco Calzolari a Joachim Camerarius II', in *Dai cantieri della storia: liber amicorum per Paolo Prodi*, ed. Gian Paolo Brizzi and Giuseppe Olmi (Bologna, 2007), pp. 343–61, here p. 360.

1 Finding His Way: The Early Years

1 Laura Laurencich-Minelli, 'From the New World to Bologna, 1533: A Gift for Pope Clement VII and Bolognese Collections of the Sixteenth and Seventeenth Centuries', *Journal of the History of Collections*, XXIV/2 (2012), pp. 145–58; Davide Domenici, 'Missionary Gift Records of Mexican Objects in Early Modern Italy', in *The New*

World in Early Modern Italy, 1492–1750, ed. Elizabeth Horodowich and Lia Markey (Cambridge, 2017), pp. 86–102.

2   Erwin Panofsky, *The Life and Art of Albrecht Dürer* (Princeton, NJ, 1955), p. 209.

3   Giuseppe Montalenti, 'Aldrovandi, Ulisse', in *Dizionario biografico degli italiani* (Rome, 1960), vol. II, pp. 118–24.

4   Girolamo Benzoni, 'Al Beatissimo et Santissimo Padre Nostro Signore Pio Quarto, Pontefice Massimo', in *La historia del Mondo Nuovo* (Venice, 1565).

5   Sandra Tugnoli Pattaro, *Metodo e sistema delle scienze nel pensiero di Ulisse Aldrovandi* (Bologna, 1981), p. 178.

6   Ibid., p. 13.

7   Alessandro Tosi, *Ulisse Aldrovandi e la Toscana: carteggio e testimonianze documentarie* (Florence, 1989), p. 416.

8   Adriano Prosperi, *L'eresia del libro grande: storia di Giorgio Siculo e della sua setta* (Milan, 2000), p. 197.

9   Katherine M. Bentz, 'Ulisse Aldrovandi, Antiquities, and the Roman Inquisition', *Sixteenth Century Journal*, XLIII/4 (2012), pp. 963–88; Margaret Daly Davis, 'Introduction' to *Ulisse Aldrovandi: Tutte le statue antiche, che in Roma in diversi luoghi, e case particolari si veggono, raccolte e descritte per Ulisse Aldroandi, . . . in Lucio Mauro: Le antichità della città di Roma . . . (Venezia 1562); Teil I: Einleitung und Volltext* (Heidelberg, 2009), pp. 4–13.

10 Lina Bolzoni, 'Parole e immagini per il ritratto di un nuovo Ulisse: L'"invenzione" dell'Aldrovandi per la sua villa di campagna', in *Documentary Culture: Florence and Rome from Grand-Duke Ferdinando I to Pope Alexander VII*, ed. Elizabeth Cropper, Giovanni Perini and Francesco Solinas (Bologna, 1992), pp. 317–48, here p. 328.

11 Peter Mason, *The Modernists that Rome Made: Turner and Other Foreign Artists in Rome XVI–XIX century* (Rome, 2020), pp. 47–55.

12 Kathleen W. Christian, *Empire without End: Antiquities Collections in Renaissance Rome, c. 1350–1527* (New Haven, CT, and London, 2010).

13 Salvatore Settis and Carlo Gasparri, *I marmi Torlonia: Collezionare capolavori*, exh. cat., Musei Capitolini, Rome (Milan, 2020), pp. 278–81.

14 Sabine Eiche, 'On the Layout of the Cesi Palace and Gardens in the Vatican Borgo', *Mitteilungen des Kunsthistorischen Institut in Florenz*, XXXIX/2–3 (1995), pp. 258–81.

15 Jean Seznec, *The Survival of the Pagan Gods: The Mythographical Tradition and Its Place in Renaissance Humanism and Art* (New York, 1953), p. 229.

He cites, in particular, *De deis gentium varia et multiplex historia in qua simul de eorum imaginibus et cognominibus agitur* (1548) by Lilio Gregori Giraldi, *Mythologiae sive explicationis fabularum libri decem* (1551) by Natale Conti and *Le imagini colla sposizione degli dei degli antichi* (1556) by Vincenzo Cartari.

16 Julia Lenaghan, 'Assessing a Roman Copy: The Story of the Syon Aphrodite', *American Journal of Archaeology*, CXXIII/1 (2019), pp. 79–100.

17 Sabine Eiche, 'Cardinal Giulio della Rovere and the Vigna Carpi', *Journal of the Society of Architectural Historians*, XLV/2 (1986), pp. 113–33.

18 Tugnoli Pattaro, *Metodo e sistema*, p. 48 n. 46; and Antonio Battistella, *Il S. Officio e la riforma religiosa in Bologna* (Bologna, 1905), p. 120 n. 1.

19 Battistella, *Il S. Officio*, pp. 187–8.

20 Francesco Ceccarelli, 'Studi di architettura di Ulisse Aldrovandi', *Annali di architettura*, XXVIII (2016), pp. 63–82.

21 Giuseppe Olmi, *Ulisse Aldrovandi: scienza e natura nel secondo cinquecento* (Trent, 1976), p. 60; Giuseppe Olmi, *L'inventario del mondo: catalogazione della natura e luoghi del sapere nella prima età moderna* (Bologna, 1992), p. 55 n. 115.

22 Damiano Acciarino, *Lettere sulle grottesche, 1580–1581* (Rome, 2018), p. 85.

23 Giovanni Fantuzzi, *Memorie della vita di Ulisse Aldrovandi* (Bologna, 1774), pp. 130–31.

24 *Tavole*, BUB, 007/1-131 and 132, 001/2-146. There are only two other antiquities represented in the *Tavole*: 007/1-008 (the famous sculpture of a chimera from Arezzo inscribed with letters in the Etruscan alphabet; see p. 74); and 007/1-126 (two fifth-century Sicilian coins from Syracusa, with thanks to Andrew McCabe for the identification).

25 *The Paper Museum of Cassiano dal Pozzo*, exh. cat., British Museum, London (1993), pp. 70–71.

2 The Network Expands

1 Sandra Tugnoli Pattaro, *Metodo e sistema delle scienze nel pensiero di Ulisse Aldrovandi* (Bologna, 1981), p. 46.

2 Laurent Pinon, 'Clématite bleue contre poissons séchées: Sept lettres inédites d'Ippolito Salviani à Ulisse Aldrovandi', *Mélanges de l'École française de Rome: Italie et la Méditerrannée*, CXIV/2 (2002), pp. 477–92, here pp. 484 and 491.

3 Florike Egmond, 'Into the Wild', in *Naturalists in the Field: Collecting, Recording and Preserving the Natural World from the Fifteenth to the Twenty-First Century*, ed. Arthur MacGregor (Leiden, 2018), pp. 166–211, esp. pp. 169–76.

4 Florike Egmond and Sachiko Kusukawa, 'Circulation of Images and Graphic Practices in the Case of Gessner', *Gesnerus: Swiss Journal of the History of Medicine and Science*, LXXIII/I (2016), pp. 29–72.

5 Alessandro Tosi, *Ulisse Aldrovandi e la Toscana: carteggio e testimonianze documentarie* (Florence, 1989), p. 200.

6 Tugnoli Pattaro, *Metodo e sistema delle scienze nel pensiero di Ulisse Aldrovandi*, p. 180.

7 Carlo Raimondi, 'Lettere di P. A. Mattioli', *Bullettino Senese di Storia Patria*, XIII/I–2 (1906), p. 146.

8 Ibid., p. 156.

9 Ibid., p. 145.

10 Fabio Garbari, Lucia Tongiorgi Tomasi and Alessandro Tosi, *Giardino dei simplici/Garden of Simples* (Pisa, 2002).

11 Elisa Andretta and José Pardo-Tomás, 'Books, Plants, Herbaria: Diego Hurtado de Mendoza and His Circle in Italy (1539–1554)', *History of Science*, LVIII/I (2020), pp. 1–25.

12 Tosi, *Ulisse Aldrovandi e la Toscana*, pp. 49–50.

13 Eugenio Turri, 'La Montagne et les passions territoriales: l'exemple du Mont Baldo (Italie)', *Revue de géographie*, LXXXII/3 (1994), pp. 31–48.

14 Francesco Calzolari, *Il viaggio di Monte Baldo*, ed. Giuseppe Sandrini (Verona, 2007), pp. 13 and 31.

15 Mario Cermenati, 'Francesco Calzolari e le sue lettere all'Aldrovandi', *Annali di Botanica*, VII/I (1908), p. 109.

16 Calzolari, *Il viaggio di Monte Baldo*, p. 46.

17 Cermenati, 'Francesco Calzolari e le sue lettere all'Aldrovandi', pp. 91–3.

18 BUB, MS 382, I, c. 164c with transcription.

19 Giuseppe Sandrini, 'Il viaggiatore della Campana d'oro', in Calzolari, *Il viaggio di Monte Baldo*, p. 75.

20 Raimondi, 'Lettere di P. A. Mattioli', p. 134.

21 Cermenati, 'Francesco Calzolari e le sue lettere all'Aldrovandi', p. 100.

22 Giuseppe Olmi, *L'inventario del mondo: catalogazione della natura e luoghi del sapere nella prima età moderna* (Bologna, 1992), p. 53 n. 110.

23 Peter Mason and José Pardo-Tomás, 'Bringing It Back from Mexico: Eleven Paintings of Trees in *I cinque libri delle piante* of Pier'Antonio

Michiel (1510–1576)', *Journal of the History of Collections*, XXXII/2 (2020), pp. 225–37.

24 Tosi, *Ulisse Aldrovandi e la Toscana*, pp. 51–4.

25 Raimondi, 'Lettere di P. A. Mattioli', p. 141.

26 L. Ciancio, 'The Many Gardens – Real, Symbolic, Visual – of Pietro Andrea Mattioli', in *From Art to Science: Experiencing Nature in the European Garden, 1500–1700*, ed. Juliette Ferdinand (Treviso, 2016), pp. 35–45.

27 BUB, MS 382, I, c. 164c and c. 165r.

28 Cermenati, 'Francesco Calzolari e le sue lettere all'Aldrovandi', p. 102.

29 Peter Mason, 'Mary's Armadillo', in *New World Objects of Knowledge: A Cabinet of Curiosities*, ed. Mark Thurner and Juan Pimentel (London, 2021), pp. 83–5.

30 Peter Mason, 'André Thevet, Pierre Belon and *Americana* in the Embroideries of Mary Queen of Scots', *Journal of the Warburg and Courtauld Institutes*, LXXVIII (2015), pp. 207–21.

31 Conrad Gessner, *Historia animalium IV* (Zurich, 1558), p. 219.

32 Cermenati, 'Francesco Calzolari e le sue lettere all'Aldrovandi', p. 129.

33 Tosi, *Ulisse Aldrovandi e la Toscana*, p. 150.

34 Sachiko Kusukawa, *Picturing the Book of Nature: Image, Text and Argument in Sixteenth-Century Human Anatomy and Medical Botany* (Chicago, IL, and London, 2012), p. 141.

35 Giovanni Fantuzzi, *Memorie della vita di Ulisse Aldrovandi* (Bologna, 1774), pp. 222–4, here p. 222.

36 Florike Egmond, 'Visual Immersion: Daniele Barbaro's Fish Album and the Wave of Interest in Aquatic Creatures in Mid-Sixteenth-Century Europe', *Notes and Records: The Royal Society Journal of the History of Science* (forthcoming).

37 Tosi, *Ulisse Aldrovandi e la Toscana*, p. 68.

38 Ibid., p. 77.

39 Pinon, 'Clématite bleue contre poissons séchées', pp. 477–92.

40 Cermenati, 'Francesco Calzolari e le sue lettere all'Aldrovandi', p. 95. See especially the classic article by Giuseppe Olmi, '"Molti amici in varij luoghi": studio della natura e rapporti epistolari nel secolo XVI', *Nuncius*, VI (1991), pp. 3–11.

41 Tosi, *Ulisse Aldrovandi e la Toscana*, p. 75.

42 Ibid., pp. 47–8.

43 Ibid., p. 230.

44 Olmi, *L'inventario del mondo*, p. 57 n. 119.

45 Tosi, *Ulisse Aldrovandi e la Toscana*, p. 207.

46 Cristina Bellorini, *The World of Plants in Renaissance Tuscany: Medicine and Botany* (Farnham, 2016), p. 55.

47 Tosi, *Ulisse Aldrovandi e la Toscana*, p. 24 n. 66.

48 Giuseppe Olmi, 'Science and the Court: Some Comments on "Patronage" in Italy', in *Science and Power: The Historical Foundations of Research Policies in Europe*, ed. Luca Guzzetti (Florence, 1994), pp. 25–45.

49 Silvio Bedini, *The Pope's Elephant* (Manchester, 1997).

50 Aldrovandi to Clusius, 15 March 1574, in Giuseppe Olmi, 'Bologna nel secolo XVI: Una capitale europea della ricerca naturalistica', in *Crocevia e capitale della migrazione artistica: forestieri a Bologna e bolognese nel mondo (secoli XV–XVI)*, ed. Sabine Frommel (Bologna, 2010), pp. 61–80, here p. 69 n. 30.

51 Raimondi, 'Lettere di P. A. Mattioli', p. 151.

52 Paula Findlen, *Possessing Nature: Museums, Collecting, and Scientific Culture in Early Modern Italy* (Berkeley and Los Angeles, CA, 1994), pp. 247–87; Giuseppe Olmi, 'Farmacopea antica e medicina moderna: la disputa sulla teriaca nel Cinquecento bolognese', *Physis*, XIX (1977), pp. 197–246.

53 Cermenati, 'Francesco Calzolari e le sue lettere all'Aldrovandi', pp. 91–2, 103, 109.

54 Tosi, *Ulisse Aldrovandi e la Toscana*, pp. 102–3.

55 Ibid., pp. 74–7.

56 Ibid., pp. 125, 128, 132, 138.

57 Ibid., pp. 177–8.

58 Baldo Falcucci to Francesco Maria II della Rovere, 24 November 1582, in Patrizia Cavazzini, *Porta Virtutis: il processo a Federico Zuccari* (Rome, 2020), p. 166.

3 Forming a Collection, Friendship and Patronage

1 Alessandro Tosi, *Ulisse Aldrovandi e la Toscana: carteggio e testimonianze documentarie* (Florence, 1989), pp. 137–8.

2 Giovanni Fantuzzi, *Memorie della vita di Ulisse Aldrovandi* (Bologna, 1774), p. 241; Giorgio Nonni, ed., *Costanzo Felici: Lettere a Ulisse Aldrovandi* (Urbino, 1982), pp. 78–82.

3 Tosi, *Ulisse Aldrovandi e la Toscana*, pp. 174–5.

4 Calzolari to Joachim Camerarius II, 20 March 1582, in Giuseppe Olmi, 'Per la storia dei rapporti scientifici fra Italia e Germania:

Le lettere di Francesco Calzolari a Joachim Camerarius II',
in *Dai cantieri della storia: liber amicorum per Paolo Prodi*, ed. Gian Paolo
Brizzi and Giuseppe Olmi (Bologna, 2007), pp. 343–61, here
p. 357.

5   15 March 1560, BUB, MS 382, I, c. 185r with transcription. Carlo
Raimondi, 'Lettere di P. A. Mattioli ad Ulisse Aldrovandi', *Bullettino
Senese di Storia Patria*, XIII/1–2 (1906), pp. 121–85, here p. 145.

6   Fantuzzi, *Memorie della vita di Ulisse Aldrovandi*, p. 237; Emanuela
Guidoboni, '17 novembre 1570: Un terremoto distruttivo al
tramonto della dinastia', in *Gli Este: Rinascimento e Barocco a Ferrara e
Modena*, ed. Stefano Casciu and Marcello Toffanello, exh. cat.,
Reggia di Venaria, Turin (Modena, 2014), pp. 160–63.

7   Paolo Boldreghini, 'Un atlante dell'avifauna selvatica italiana ed
europea del Cinquecento e degli "esotici" dai nuovi mondi', in *Natura
picta: Ulisse Aldrovandi*, ed. Alessandro Alessandrini and Alessandro
Ceregato (Bologna, 2007), pp. 79–82.

8   Mario Cermenati, 'Francesco Calzolari e le sue lettere
all'Aldrovandi', *Annali di Botanica*, VII/1 (1908), p. 97.

9   Ibid., p. 105.

10 Tosi, *Ulisse Aldrovandi e la Toscana*, p. 140.

11 Ibid., pp. 185–7.

12 Ibid., p. 231.

13 BUB, MS 382, I, c. 181r with transcription.

14 Cermenati, 'Francesco Calzolari e le sue lettere all'Aldrovandi',
p. 130.

15 Tosi, *Ulisse Aldrovandi e la Toscana*, p. 17.

16 Ibid., pp. 118–19.

17 Ibid., pp. 130–31.

18 Ibid., pp. 123–7.

19 Ibid., p. 111.

20 Ibid., pp. 84–7.

21 Lucia Tongiorgi Tomasi, 'Art and Nature in the *Giardino dei semplici*:
From its Origins to the End of the Medici Dynasty', in Fabio
Garbari, Lucia Tongiorgi Tomasi and Alessandro Tosi, *Giardino dei
semplici/Garden of Simples* (Pisa, 2002), pp. 149–88, here p. 155.

22 Tosi, *Ulisse Aldrovandi e la Toscana*, pp. 81–3, 93.

23 Laurent Pinon, 'Clématite bleue contre poissons séchées: sept lettres
inédites d'Ippolito Salviani à Ulisse Aldrovandi', *Mélanges de l'École
française de Rome: Italie et la Méditerrannée*, CXIV/2 (2002), pp. 477–92,
here pp. 486 and 491.

24 Cermenati, 'Francesco Calzolari e le sue lettere all'Aldrovandi', p. 126; Tosi, *Ulisse Aldrovandi e la Toscana*, p. 77.

25 Cermenati, 'Francesco Calzolari e le sue lettere all'Aldrovandi', p. III.

26 Tosi, *Ulisse Aldrovandi e la Toscana*, p. 240.

27 BUB, MS 382, I, c. 145r with transcription.

28 Cermenati, 'Francesco Calzolari e le sue lettere all'Aldrovandi', p. 127.

29 Giovanni Battista De Toni, 'Spigolature Aldrovandiane', *Madonna Verona*, I (1907), pp. 18–26; Gianni Peretti, 'I dipinti per lo studiolo di Giulio Della Torre', in *Caroto: Giovan Francesco Caroto, 1480 circa–1555*, ed. Francesca Rossi, Gianni Peretti and Edoardo Rossetti (Milan, 2021), pp. 140–43.

30 Alessandro Tosi, 'Acconciare, saccare, dipingere: Pratiche di rappresentazione della natura tra le "spigolature" Aldrovandiane', in *Ulisse Aldrovandi: libri e immagini di storia naturale nella prima età moderna*, ed. Giuseppe Olmi and Fulvio Simoni (Bologna, 2018), pp. 49–58.

31 Raimondi, 'Lettere di P. A. Mattioli ad Ulisse Aldrovandi', p. 145.

32 Florike Egmond, *The World of Carolus Clusius: Natural History in the Making, 1550–1610* (London, 2010), p. 18.

33 Aldrovandi to Clusius, 8 February 1569, Leiden University Library, VUL 101.

34 Carolus Clusius, *Aromatum et simplicium aliquot medicamentorum apud Indos nascentium historia* (Antwerp, 1567).

35 Carolus Clusius, *Rariorum aliquot stirpium per Hispanias observatarum historia* (Antwerp, 1576).

36 Alberta Campitelli, *Gli horti dei Papi: i giardini vaticani dal medioevo al novecento* (Milan, 2009), p. IIO.

37 Fantuzzi, *Memorie della vita di Ulisse Aldrovandi*, pp. 249–50.

38 Codex Kentmann, 'Observationes', fol. 31v, Anna Amalia Bibliothek, Weimar. See Sachiko Kusukawa, 'Image, Text and *Observatio*: The *Codex Kentmanus*', *Early Science and Medicine*, XIV (2009), pp. 445–75, here p. 452.

39 Olmi, 'Per la storia dei rapporti scientifici fra Italia e Germania', p. 351.

40 Fantuzzi, *Memorie della vita di Ulisse Aldrovandi*, p. 253.

41 Claudia Lazzaro, 'Animals as Cultural Signs: A Medici Menagerie in the Grotto at Castello', in *Reframing the Renaissance: Visual Culture in Europe and Latin America, 1450–1650*, ed. Claire Farago (New Haven, CT, and London, 1995), pp. 197–227; Angelica Groom, *Exotic Animals in the Art and Culture of the Medici Court in Florence* (Leiden, 2018).

42   Sheila Barker, 'Cosimo I de' Medici and the Renaissance Sciences:
     "To measure and to see"', in *A Companion to Cosimo I de' Medici*,
     ed. Alessio Assonitis and Henk Th. van Veen (Leiden, 2022),
     pp. 520–80.

43   Michel de Montaigne, *Oeuvres complètes*, ed. Albert Thibaudet and
     Maurice Rat (Paris, 1962), p. 1198.

44   Mauro Cristofani, 'Il "mito" etrusco in Europa fra XVI e XVIII
     secolo', in *Gli Etruschi*, ed. Massimo Pallottino (Milan, 1992),
     pp. 218–31.

45   Anna Maria Massinelli, 'La Collection des Médicis au temps de
     Cosme Ier et de François Ier', in *Trésors des Médicis*, ed. Cristina
     Acidini Luchinat (Paris, 1998), pp. 53–72.

46   Agostino Lapini, *Diario Fiorentino dal 252 al 1596*, ed. Giuseppe Odoardo
     Corazzini (Florence, 1900), p. 258.

47   Tosi, *Ulisse Aldrovandi e la Toscana*, p. 205.

48   Ibid., p. 208.

49   Ibid., pp. 205–6.

50   Ibid., p. 208.

51   Ibid., pp. 224–5.

52   Ibid., p. 278.

53   Ibid., p. 419.

54   Ibid., p. 226.

55   Ibid., p. 263.

56   Ibid., p. 267.

57   Ibid., p. 225.

58   Ibid., p. 253; Fantuzzi, *Memorie della vita di Ulisse Aldrovandi*, pp. 257–60.

59   Tosi, *Ulisse Aldrovandi e la Toscana*, pp. 281–3.

60   Egmond, *The World of Carolus Clusius*.

61   Tosi, *Ulisse Aldrovandi e la Toscana*, p. 290.

62   Ibid., p. 209.

63   E. van Kessel, *The Lives of Paintings: Presence, Agency and Likeness in Venetian
     Art of the Sixteenth Century* (Berlin and Boston, MA, 2017), p. 187.

64   ORN, I; Tosi, *Ulisse Aldrovandi e la Toscana*, pp. 305–7.

4 The American Mirage

1   Laura Laurencich-Minelli, 'From the New World to Bologna,
    1533: A Gift to Pope Clement VII and Bolognese Collections of
    the Sixteenth and Seventeenth Centuries', *Journal of the History of
    Collections*, XXIV/2 (2012), pp. 145–58, here p. 157 n. 29.

2 Giuseppe Olmi, *L'inventario del mondo: catalogazione della natura e luoghi del sapere nella prima età moderna* (Bologna, 1992), p. 37 n. 53.

3 Juan Páez de Castro, 26 October 1546, in Arantxa Domingo Malvadi, *Bibliofilia humanista en tiempos de Felipe II: la biblioteca de Juan Páez de Castro* (Salamanca, 2011), p. 354.

4 Geoffrey Eatough, *Fracastoro's 'Syphilis'*, with introduction, text, translation and notes (Liverpool, 1984).

5 Massimo Donattini, 'Orizzonti geografici dell'editoria italiana (1493–1560)', in *Il Nuovo Mondo nella coscienza italiana e tedesca del Cinquecento*, ed. Adriano Prosperi and Wolfgang Reinhard (Bologna, 1992), pp. 79–154.

6 Alessandro Tosi, *Ulisse Aldrovandi e la Toscana: carteggio e testimonianze documentarie* (Florence, 1989), p. 190.

7 Giuseppe Gabriele, *Il carteggio linceo* (Rome, 1996), p. 1163.

8 Damiano Acciarino, *Lettere sulle grottesche, 1580–1581* (Rome, 2018), p. 89.

9 Pedro de Cieza de León, *Segunda parte de la Crónica del Perú* (Madrid, 1880), p. 107.

10 José Pardo-Tomás, 'Making Natural History in New Spain, 1525–1590', in *The Globalization of Knowledge in the Iberian Colonial World*, ed. Helga Wendt (Berlin, 2016), pp. 29–51.

11 Sabina Brevaglieri, *Natural desiderio di sapere: Roma barocca fra vecchi e nuovi mondi* (Rome, 2019), p. 42.

12 Agustín Farfán, *Tratado breve de medicina*, ed. M. Cortés Guadarrama (Madrid, 2020).

13 Olmi, *L'inventario del mondo*, p. 228.

14 Emma Sallent Del Colombo and José Pardo-Tomás, 'Materiali aldrovandiani in Spagna: l'enigmatico caso del *Códice Pomar*', in *Ulisse Aldrovandi: Libri e immagini di storia naturale nella prima età moderna*, ed. Giuseppe Olmi and Fulvio Simoni (Bologna, 2018), pp. 37–48, here p. 42.

15 Peter Mason and José Pardo-Tomás, 'Bringing It Back from Mexico: Eleven Paintings of Trees in *I cinque libri delle piante* of Pier'Antonio Michiel (1510–1576)', *Journal of the History of Collections*, XXXII/2 (2020), pp. 225–37.

16 Paula Findlen, *Possessing Nature: Museums, Collecting, and Scientific Culture in Early Modern Italy* (Berkeley and Los Angeles, CA, 1994), pp. 17–23.

17 Sandra Tugnoli Pattaro, *Metodo e sistema delle scienze nel pensiero di Ulisse Aldrovandi* (Bologna, 1981), pp. 175–232.

18 Tosi, *Ulisse Aldrovandi e la Toscana*, pp. 294–5.

19 Sallent Del Colombo and Pardo-Tomás, 'Materiali aldrovandiani in Spagna', p. 44.

20 Findlen, *Possessing Nature*, p. 75.

21 Giuseppe Olmi, 'Ulisse Aldrovandi e la natura del Nuovo Mondo', in *Tesoro Mexicano: visioni della natura fra Vecchio e Nuovo Mondo*, ed. Giorgio Antei (Parma, 2015), pp. 181–93.

22 Giuseppe Gabriele, *Contributi alla storia della Accademia dei Lincei* (Rome, 1989), pp. 731–4.

23 Tosi, *Ulisse Aldrovandi e la Toscana*, p. 428.

24 Paul Vandenbroeck, 'Amerindian Art and Ornamental Objects in Royal Collections: Brussels, Mechelen, Duurstede, 1520–1530', in *America: Bride of the Sun*, exh. cat., Royal Museum of Fine Arts, Antwerp (Ghent, 1991), pp. 99–119.

25 Peter Mason, 'From Presentation to Representation: *Americana* in Europe', *Journal of the History of Collections*, VI/1 (1994), pp. 1–20.

26 Mario Cermenati, 'Francesco Calzolari e le sue lettere all'Aldrovandi', *Annali di Botanica*, VII (1909), pp. 83–132, here p. 104.

27 Borgarutio Borgarucci, 'To the Readers', preface to *Delle cose che si portano dall'Indie Occidentali pertinenti all'vso della medicina: Raccolte, & trattate dal Dottor Nicolò Monardes, medico di Siuiglia* (Venice, 1589).

28 Michel Hochmann, ed., *Il sogno di un cardinale: collezioni e artisti di Ferdinando de' Medici*, exh. cat., Accademia di Francia, Rome (1999), pp. 222 and 65 n. 39.

29 Alessandro Tosi, 'Contrivances of Art: The Power of Imagery in the Early Modern Culture of Curiosity', in *Fakes!?: Hoaxes, Counterfeits and Deception in Early Modern Science*, ed. Marco Beretta and Maria Conforti (Sagamore Beach, MA, 2014), pp. 153–75, here p. 170.

30 Peter Mason, 'André Thevet, Pierre Belon and *Americana* in the Embroideries of Mary Queen of Scots', *Journal of the Warburg and Courtauld Institutes*, LXXVIII (2015), pp. 207–21.

31 Paul J. Smith, 'On Toucans and Hornbills: Readings in Early Modern Ornithology from Belon to Buffon', in *Early Modern Zoology: The Construction of Animals in Science, Literature and the Visual Arts*, ed. Karl A. E. Enenkel and Paul J. Smith (Leiden, 2007), pp. 75–119.

32 Peter Mason, *Infelicities: Representations of the Exotic* (Baltimore, MD, and London, 1998), pp. 16–41. Alessandro Cecchi, Lucilia Conigliello and Marzia Faietti, eds, *Jacopo Ligozzi 'pittore universalissimo'*, exh. cat., Palazzo Pitti, Florence (Livorno, 2014), p. 120.

33 Stefan Hanß, 'Making Featherwork in Early Modern Europe', and Ulinka Rublack, 'Performing America: Featherwork and Affective

Politics', in *Materialised Identities in Early Modern Culture, 1450–1750*, ed. Susanna Burghartz et al. (Amsterdam, 2021), pp. 137–85 and 187–229 respectively; Stefan Hanß and Ulinka Rublack, 'Knowledge Production, Image Networks, and the Material Significance of Feathers in Late Humanist Heidelberg', *Renaissance Quarterly*, LXXIV/2 (2021), pp. 412–53.

34 Laura Laurencich-Minelli, ed., *Bologna e il Mondo Nuovo*, exh. cat., Museo Civico Medievale, Bologna (1992), pp. 138–9.

35 Theodore De Bry, *Secunda Pars Americae* (Frankfurt, 1591); Christian F. Feest, 'European Collecting of American Indian Artefacts and Art', *Journal of the History of Collections*, V/1 (1993), pp. 1–11; Lia Markey, 'Aldrovandi's New World Natives in Bologna (or How to Draw the Unseen *al vivo*)', in *The New World in Early Modern Italy, 1492–1750*, ed. Elizabeth Horodowich and Lia Markey (Cambridge, 2017), pp. 225–47.

36 André Thevet, *Cosmographie universelle* (Paris, 1575), vol. II, fols 924r and 955v. For the engravings in Thevet's *Les Vrais Pourtraits et vies des hommes illustres grecz, latins, et payens: recueillliz de leurs tableaux livres, medalles antiques, et modernes* (Paris, 1584), see Peter Mason, *The Lives of Images* (London, 2001), p. 107.

37 Davide Domenici, 'Rediscovery of a Mesoamerican Greenstone Sculpture from the Collection of Ulisse Aldrovandi', *Journal of the History of Collections*, XXXIV/1 (2022), pp. 1–22.

38 Laura Laurencich-Minelli, 'Bologna e il Mondo Nuovo', in *Bologna e il Mondo Nuovo*, pp. 9–23; Davide Domenici, 'Handling Sacrifice: Reception and Perception of Mesoamerican Knives in Early Modern Italy', in *Missionary Objects and Collecting (16th–20th Centuries)*, ed. Sabina Brevaglieri, *Quaderni storici* (forthcoming).

39 Davide Domenici, 'Mesoamerican Mosaics from Early European Collections: Style, Provenance and Provenience', *Estudios de Cultura Náhuatl*, LIX (2020), pp. 7–65.

40 Feest, 'European Collecting of American Indian Artefacts and Art', p. 3.

41 Michel de Montaigne, 'Des Cannibales', in *Oeuvres complètes*, ed. Albert Thibaudet and Maurice Rat (Paris, 1962), p. 206.

42 Andrea Ubrizsy Savoia, 'Le piante americane nell'Erbario di Ulisse Aldrovandi', *Webbia*, XLVIII (1993), pp. 579–98.

43 Giovanni Fantuzzi, *Memorie della vita di Ulisse Aldrovandi* (Bologna, 1774), p. 207.

44 Laurent Pinon, 'Clématite bleue contre poissons séchées: sept lettres inédites d'Ippolito Salviani à Ulisse Aldrovandi', *Mélanges de l'École*

française de Rome: Italie et la Méditerrannée, CXIV/2 (2002), pp. 477–92, here pp. 487 and 492.

45 Tosi, *Ulisse Aldrovandi e la Toscana*, p. 294.

46 Dario Franchini et al., eds, *La scienza a corte: collezionismo eclettico, natura e immagine a Mantova fra Rinascimento e manierismo* (Rome, 1979), p. 22; Giuseppe Olmi, '"Things of Nature" from the New World in the Early Modern Bologna Collections', in *Images Take Flight: Feather Art in Mexico and Europe, 1400–1700*, ed. Alessandra Russo et al. (Munich, 2015), pp. 138–48. Ubrizsy Savoia, 'Le piante americane dell'Erbario di Ulisse Aldrovandi'.

47 Tosi, *Ulisse Aldrovandi e la Toscana*, p. 271.

48 Peter Mason, *Before Disenchantment: Images of Exotic Animals and Plants in the Early Modern World* (London, 2009), p. 87.

49 See also Irina Podgorny, 'Animal Remedies in Space and Time: The Case of the Nail of the Great Beast', in *Knowledge in Translation: Global Patterns of Scientific Exchange, 1000–1800 CE*, ed. Patrick Manning and Abigail Owen (Pittsburgh, PA, 2018), pp. 149–63.

50 Cristina Brito, 'The Monstrous in Aldrovandi and the Natural Order of Marine Animals in the 16th and 17th Centuries', in *Natureza, causalidade e formas de corporeidade*, ed. Adelino Cardoso, Manuel Silvério Marques and Marta Mendonça (Lisbon, 2016), pp. 177–92.

51 Florike Egmond and Peter Mason, eds, *The Whale Book: Whales and Other Marine Animals as Described by Adriaen Coenen in 1585* (London, 2003), pp. 116–17; Florike Egmond and Peter Mason, 'Armadillos in Unlikely Places: Some Unpublished Sixteenth-Century Sources for New World *Rezeptionsgeschichte* in Northern Europe', *Ibero-Amerikanisches Archiv*, XX/1–2 (1994), pp. 3–52.

52 Olmi, *L'inventario del mondo*, pp. 238–9.

53 Tosi, *Ulisse Aldrovandi e la Toscana*, pp. 254–8.

54 Ibid., p. 308.

55 Ibid., p. 224.

56 Conrad Gessner, *Nomenclatur aquatilium animantium* (Zurich, 1560), p. 92.

57 Geoffrey Eatough, ed., *Selections from Peter Martyr* (Turnhout, 1998), p. 65 (English) and pp. 151–2 (Latin).

58 Laura Larencich-Minelli, *Un 'giornale' del Cinquecento sulla scoperta dell'America: Il manoscritto di Ferrara* (Milan, 1985), pp. 57–8.

59 Florike Egmond, *Eye for Detail: Images of Plants and Animals in Art and Science, 1500–1630* (London, 2017), p. 104.

60 Paul Hulton, *America 1585: The Complete Drawings of John White* (Chapel Hill, NC, 1984), pp. 73 and 181.

5 Anomalies

1 Alessandro Tosi, *Ulisse Aldrovandi e la Toscana: carteggio e testimonianze
   documentarie* (Florence, 1989), pp. 286, 330 and 340.
2 *Tavole*, BUB, 005/1-24.
3 Bartolomeo Ambrosini, *Paralipomena accuratissima historiæ omnium
   animalium*, appended to MH, p. 135.
4 Mary Beagon, ed., *The Elder Pliny on the Human Animal: Natural History
   Book 7* (Oxford, 2005).
5 John B. Friedman, *The Monstrous Races in Medieval Art and Thought*
   (Cambridge and London, 1981); Florike Egmond and Peter Mason,
   The Mammoth and the Mouse: Microhistory and Morphology (Baltimore, MD,
   and London, 1997), pp. 105–32.
6 Peter Mason, *Deconstructing America: Representations of the Other* (London
   and New York, 1990), pp. 80 and 120.
7 Ibid., pp. 97–117; Peter Mason, *The Ways of the World: European
   Representations of Other Cultures from Homer to Sade* (Canon Pyon,
   Herefordshire, 2015).
8 Jean Céard, *La nature et les prodiges: L'Insolite au XVIe siècle* (Geneva,
   1996), pp. 455–7.
9 Ambroise Paré, *Des monstres et prodiges*, ed. Jean Céard (Geneva, 1971).
10 Ambrosini, *Paralipomena*, Appendix to MH, p. 154.
11 Peter Mason, *Before Disenchantment: Images of Exotic Animals and Plants in
   the Early Modern World* (London, 2009), pp. 87–123.
12 See also Paul J. Smith, 'On Toucans and Hornbills: Readings in
   Early Modern Ornithology from Belon to Buffon', in *Early Modern
   Zoology: The Construction of Animals in Science, Literature and the Visual
   Arts*, ed. Karl A. E. Enenkel and Paul J. Smith (Leiden, 2007),
   pp. 75–119.
13 Mason, *Before Disenchantment*, pp. 134–5.
14 José Ramón Marcaida López, *Arte y ciencia en el barroco español*
   (Madrid, 2014), pp. 222–31; José Ramón Marcaida López, 'Echoes
   of Aldrovandi: Notes on an Illustrated Album from the Natural
   History Museum in London', in *Ulisse Aldrovandi: libri e immagini di storia
   natura nella prima età moderna*, ed. Giuseppe Olmi and Fulvio Simoni
   (Bologna, 2018), pp. 23–7.
15 Philip Morel, *Les grotesques: les figures de l'imaginaire dans la peinture italienne
   de la fin de la Renaissance* (Paris, 1997), p. 74.
16 *Liber monstrorum*, I: 22, 'De barbosis mulieribus' or 'De mulieribus
   barbatis'. There are two modern editions: Corrado Bologna,

Liber monstrorum de diversis generibus: libro delle mirabili difformità (Milan, 1977), and Franco Porsia, *Liber monstrorum (secolo IX)* (Naples, 2012).

17 Adam of Bremen, *Gesta Hammaburgensis ecclesiae pontificum*, IV.32; Thomas of Cantimpré, *Liber de natura rerum*, III: V, 19. Other examples in Claude Lecouteux, *Les monstres dans la littérature allemande du Moyen Age* (Göppingen, 1982), vol. II, pp. 30–31.

18 Hartmann Schedel, *Weltchronik* (Nuremberg, 1493), p. xii. The 1,809 woodcut engravings are by Michael Wohlgemut and Wilhelm Pleydenwurff.

19 Paré, *Des monstres et prodiges*, pp. 29–30; Michel de Montaigne, 'Journal de voyage en Italie', in *Oeuvres complètes*, ed. Albert Thibaudet and Maurice Rat (Paris, 1962), pp. 1118–19, with reference to Paré.

20 Montaigne, *Oeuvres complètes*, p. 96.

21 Francisco Hernández, commentary on Pliny, *Historia naturalis*, VII.16, in *Obras completas de Francisco Hernández* (Mexico, 2015), vol. IV.

22 *Tavole*, BUB, 006/2/70; Giuseppe Olmi and Lucia Tongiorgi Tomasi, 'Raffigurazione della natura e collezionismo enciclopedico nel secondo Cinquecento tra Milano e l'Europe', in *Arcimboldo: artista milanese tra Leonardo e Caravaggio*, ed. Sylvia Ferino-Pagden, exh. cat., Palazzo Reale, Milan (2011), pp. 113–49, here pp. 141–2.

23 Roberto Zapperi, *Il selvaggio gentiluomo: l'incredibile storia di Pedro Gonzalez e dei suoi figli* (Rome, 2005); Peter Mason, 'Le donne barbute di Ulisse Aldrovandi', in *Ulisse Aldrovandi: libri e immagini di storia natura nella prima età moderna*, ed. Giuseppe Olmi and Fulvio Simoni (Bologna, 2018), pp. 29–36.

24 Jerónimo Münzer, *Viaje por España y Portugal, 1494–1495*, ed. Ramón Alba (Madrid, 1991), pp. 43–5.

25 Tosi, *Ulisse Aldrovandi e la Toscana*, p. 424.

26 Paula Findlen, *Possessing Nature: Museums, Collecting, and Scientific Culture in Early Modern Italy* (Berkeley and Los Angeles, CA, 1994), pp. 17–23.

27 Aby Warburg, *The Renewal of Pagan Antiquity* [1920] (Los Angeles, CA, 1999), p. 635.

28 Robert W. Scribner, *For the Sake of Simple Folk: Popular Propaganda for the German Reformation* (Oxford, 1994), p. 132.

29 Myriam Marrache-Gouraud, *La légende des objets: Le cabinet de curiosités réfléchi par son catalogue, Europe, XVIe–XVIIe siècles* (Geneva, 2020), pp. 367–76.

30 Scribner, *For the Sake of Simple Folk*, pp. 169–75.

31 Klaus Barthelmess, 'Neue Erkenntnisse zur Walstrandungsgraphik des 16. Jahrhunderts: Erster Nachtrag zu "Monstrum horrendum"', *Deutsches Schiffahrtsarchiv*, XXI (1998), pp. 157–81.
32 Paré, *Des Monstres et prodiges*, p. 142.
33 Paolo Galluzzi, *The Lynx and the Telescope: The Parallel Worlds of Federico Cesi and Galileo* (Leiden, 2017), pp. 1–24 and 142–52.
34 Leon Battista Alberti, *Della pittura e della statua* (Milan, 1804), pp. 107–8.
35 Sharon Fermor, *Piero di Cosimo: Fiction, Invention and Fantasia* (London, 1993), pp. 16–20.
36 Juliette Ferdinand, *Bernard Palissy: Artisan des réformes entre art, science et foi* (Berlin and Boston, MA, 2019), pp. 264–6.
37 Peter Paul Rubens, *The Letters of Peter Paul Rubens*, ed. Ruth Saunders Magurn (Cambridge, 1955), p. 247 (letter of 23 March 1628).
38 *Tavole*, BUB, 007/1-68.
39 Ibid., 007/1-66.
40 Peter Mason, 'La imagen realizada por mano no humana. Sobre el tratado *Museo pictórico y escala óptica* de Antonio Palomino', in *Imagen y discurso técnico-científico en español: Miradas interdisciplinarias*, ed. Matteo De Beni (Mantua, 2019), pp. 109–36.
41 Florike Egmond and Peter Mason, eds, *The Whale Book: Whales and Other Marine Animals as Described by Adriaen Coenen in 1585* (London, 2003), pp. 8–9.
42 *Tavole*, BUB, 005/1-142.
43 Pierre Belon, *La nature et diversité des poissons* (Paris, 1555), p. 139.
44 Conrad Gessner, *De rerum fossilium, lapidum et gemmarum maxime, figuris et similitudinibus liber* (Zurich, 1565), p. 162; Urs B. Leu, *Conrad Gessner (1516–1565): Universalgelehrter und Naturforscher der Renaissance* (Zurich, 2016), pp. 367–78; Walter Etter, 'Conrad Gessner als Paläontologe', in *Facetten eines Universums: Conrad Gessner, 1516–2016*, ed. Urs B. Leu and Mylène Ruoss (Zurich, 2016), pp. 175–84.
45 Sebastian Münster, *Cosmographei* (Basel, 1550), p. 578.
46 Juliette Ferdinand, 'Le grotte rustiche di villa Della Torre nel contesto dei dibattiti scientifici del Cinquecento', *Annuario Storico della Valpolicella*, XXXIII (2016–17), pp. 71–90.
47 Lorenzo Sorbini, *La collezione Baja di pesci e piante fossili di Bolca* (Verona, 1983), p. 7; Roberto Zorzin, *Rocce e fossili del monte Baldo e dei monti Lessini veronesi* (Verona, 2016), p. 90.
48 On this debate see Martin J. S. Rudwick, *The Meaning of Fossils* (Chicago, IL, 1985), pp. 1–48; Luca Ciancio, *Esploratori del tempo profondo: scienza, storia e società nella cultura veneta dell'età moderna* (Verona, 2014), pp. 13–28;

Alessandro Ottaviani, 'The Opposite Poles of a Debate – *Lapides figurati* and the Accademia dei Lincei', *Substantia*, V/1 (2021), pp. 19–28.

49 Joseph Robertson, ed., *Inventaires de la royne descosse douairiere de France: Catalogues of the Jewels, Dresses, Furniture, Books, and Paintings of Mary Queen of Scots, 1556–1569* (Edinburgh, 1863), p. 17; André Thevet, *Cosmographie de Levant* (Lyon, 1556), p. 208.

50 Carlo Raimondi, 'Lettere di P. A. Mattioli', *Bullettino Senese di Storia Patria*, XIII/1–2 (1906), p. 154.

51 Tosi, *Ulisse Aldrovandi e la Toscana*, p. 309.

52 Mario Cermenati, 'Francesco Calzolari e le sue lettere all'Aldrovandi', *Annali di Botanica*, VII/1 (1908), p. 122.

53 Tosi, *Ulisse Aldrovandi e la Toscana*, p. 208.

54 Ibid., p. 215.

55 *In lapide depictum: pintura italiana sobre piedra, 1530–1555*, exh. cat., Museo del Prado, Madrid (2018); Johanna B. Lohff, *Malerei auf Stein: Antonio Tempestas Bilder auf Stein im Kontext der Kunst- und Naturtheorie seiner Zeit* (Munich, 2015); Mason, 'La imagen realizada por mano no humana'.

6 Art and Artists

1 Damiano Acciarino, *Lettere sulle grottesche, 1580–1581* (Rome, 2018), p. 88.

2 Giuseppe Olmi, *L'inventario del mondo: catalogazione della natura e luoghi del sapere nella prima età moderna* (Bologna, 1992), p. 123; Irene Baldriga, *L'occhio della lince: i primi Lincei tra arte, scienza e collezionismo, 1603–1630* (Rome, 2002), p. 8.

3 Gonzalo Fernández de Oviedo y Valdés, 'Prohemio', in *Historia general y natural de las Indias*, ed. José Amador de los Ríos (Madrid, 1851), Part 1, Book 10, p. 362.

4 Alessandro Tosi, *Ulisse Aldrovandi e la Toscana: carteggio e testimonianze documentarie* (Florence, 1989), pp. 338–9.

5 Ibid., p. 163.

6 Ibid., p. 156.

7 Ibid., p. 170.

8 Ibid., p. 179.

9 Daniel Hess, 'Into the Wild', in *The Early Dürer*, ed. Daniel Hess and Thomas Eser, exh. cat., Germanisches Nationalmuseum, Nuremberg (London and New York, 2012), pp. 516–20.

10 Arianne Faber Kolb, *Jan Brueghel the Elder: The Entry of the Animals into Noah's Ark* (Los Angeles, CA, 2005), p. 70.

11 Giovanni Fantuzzi, *Memorie della vita di Ulisse Aldrovandi* (Bologna, 1774), p. 254.

12 Tosi, *Ulisse Aldrovandi e la Toscana*, p. 308.

13 Carlo Raimondi, 'Lettere di P. A. Mattioli ad Ulisse Aldrovandi', *Bullettino Senese di Storia Patria*, XIII/1–2 (1906), p. 168.

14 Tosi, *Ulisse Aldrovandi e la Toscana*, p. 320.

15 Marinela Haxhiraj, *Ulisse Aldrovandi: il museografo* (Bologna, 2016), pp. 17–22.

16 Tosi, *Ulisse Aldrovandi e la Toscana*, p. 211.

17 Ibid., p. 275.

18 Giuseppe Olmi and Lucia Tongiorgi Tomasi, *De piscibus: la bottega artistica di Ulisse Aldrovandi e l'immagine naturalistica* (Rome, 1993), p. 20.

19 Lee Hendrix, 'Natural History Illustration at the Court of Rudolf II', in *Rudolf II and Prague*, ed. Eliska Fučíková et al., exh. cat., Prague Castle (London, 1997), pp. 157–71, here p. 166.

20 *Tavole*, BUB, 005/1-20, 006/2-86 and 006/2-87; Giuseppe Olmi and Lucia Tongiorgi Tomasi, 'Raffigurazione della natura e collezionismo enciclopedico nel secondo Cinquecento tra Milano e l'Europe', in *Arcimboldo: Artista milanese tra Leonardo e Caravaggio*, ed. Sylvia Ferino-Pagden, exh. cat., Palazzo Reale, Milan (2011), pp. 113–49, here pp. 134–6.

21 Thomas Dacosta Kaufmann, *Arcimboldo: Visual Jokes, Natural History, and Still-Life Painting* (Chicago, IL, and London, 2009), p. 123.

22 Della Sirena to Aldrovandi, 4 October 1573, in Dario Franchini et al., eds, *La scienza a corte: collezionismo eclettico, natura e immagine a Mantova fra Rinascimento e manierismo* (Rome, 1979), p. 230.

23 Acciarino, *Lettere sulle grottesche*, p. 104.

24 Giuseppe Olmi, *L'inventario del mondo: catalogazione della natura e luoghi del sapere nella prima età moderna* (Bologna, 1992), p. 129.

25 Ibid., p. 108 n. 291.

26 Tosi, *Ulisse Aldrovandi e la Toscana*, pp. 244–5; Peter Mason and José Pardo-Tomás, 'Bringing It Back from Mexico: Eleven Paintings of Trees in *I cinque libri delle piante* of Pier'Antonio Michiel, 1510–1576', *Journal of the History of Collections*, XXXII/2 (2020), pp. 225–37.

27 Tosi, *Ulisse Aldrovandi e la Toscana*, p. 241.

28 Ibid., p. 20 n. 55.

29 Ibid., p. 173.

30 Mario Cermenati, 'Francesco Calzolari e le sue lettere all'Aldrovandi', *Annali di Botanica*, VII/1 (1908), p. 115.

31 Ibid., p. 126.

32 Ibid., p. 128.

33 Lucilia Conigliello, 'La vita e le opere', in *Jacopo Ligozzi 'pittore universalissimo'*, ed. Alessandro Cecchi, Lucilia Conigliello and Marzia Faietti, exh. cat., Palazzo Pitti, Florence (Livorno, 2014), pp. 13–18.

34 Tosi, *Ulisse Aldrovandi e la Toscana*, p. 205.

35 Ibid., p. 351 (emphasis added).

36 Ibid., pp. 315–22.

37 Maria Elena De Luca, 'Jacopo Ligozzi: Metamorfosi del naturale', in *Jacopo Ligozzi, 'altro Apelle'*, ed. Maria Elena De Luca and Marzia Faietti, exh. cat., Uffizi Gallery, Florence (2014), pp. 31–81, here p. 48.

38 Cecchi et al., *Jacopo Ligozzi 'pittore universalissimo'*, pp. 108 and 140–41.

39 Lucia Tongiorgi Tomasi, *The Flowering of Florence: Botanical Art for the Medici* (Washington, DC, 2002), pp. 38–51.

40 Andrea Cesalpino, *De plantis libri XVI* (Florence, 1583), dedication: 'Serenissimo Francisco Medici Magno Aetruriae Duci'.

41 Pietro Castelli, *Exactissima descriptio rariorum quarundam plantarum, quae continentur Romae in Horto Farnesiano* (Rome, 1625); Cecchi et al., *Jacopo Ligozzi 'pittore universalissimo'*, pp. 70–71.

42 Acciarino, *Lettere sulle grottesche*, p. 99.

43 Tosi, *Ulisse Aldrovandi e la Toscana*, pp. 332–4.

44 Olmi, *L'inventario del mondo*, p. 63.

45 Lucia Tongiorgi Tomasi, 'Tutte le pitture dipinte al vivo dal signor Jacomo Ligozzi, a' quali non mancha se non il spirito', in *Jacopo Ligozzi 'pittore universalissimo'*, pp. 29–37, here p. 31.

46 Tosi, *Ulisse Aldrovandi e la Toscana*, p. 387.

47 Francesco Solinas, '"Tout le savoir du monde": La Correspondance Peiresc–Pasqualini', in *La Correspondance de Nicolas-Claude Fabri de Peiresc avec Lelio Pasqualini, 1601–1611, et son neveu Pompeo, 1613–1622*, ed. Veronica Carpita and Elena Vaiani (Paris, 2012), pp. ix–xviii.

48 Francesco Solinas, 'Percorsi puteani: note naturalistiche ed inediti appunti antiquari', in *Cassiano dal Pozzo: atti del seminario internazionale di studi*, ed. Francesco Solinas (Rome, 1989), pp. 95–129, here p. 98 n. 17.

49 Lucia Tongiorgi Tomasi, 'Art and Nature in the *giardino dei semplici*: From its Origins to the End of the Medici Dynasty', in Fabio Garbari, Lucia Tongiorgi Tomasi and Alessandro Tosi, *Giardino dei semplici/Garden of Simples* (Pisa, 2002), pp. 149–88, here pp. 156–7.

50 Ibid., pp. 157–8.

51 Tosi, *Ulisse Aldrovandi e la Toscana*, p. 429.

52 *Tavole*, BUB, 001/2-60.

53 Christine Kleiter, 'Birds, Colour, and Feet: A "Naif Portrait" of the Brazilian Tanager in Pierre Belon's *L'Histoire de la nature des oyseaux* (1555)', *Journal of the LUCAS Graduate Conference*, VIII (2020), pp. 6–29.

54 Olmi, *L'inventario del mondo*, p. 36 n. 52. Donatella L. Sparti, *Le collezioni dal Pozzo: storia di una famiglia e del suo museo nella Roma seicentesca* (Modena, 1992), pp. 121 and 159.

55 Acciarino, *Lettere sulle grottesche*, pp. 95–6.

56 Lina Bolzoni, 'Parole e immagini per il ritratto di un nuovo Ulisse: L'"invenzione" dell'Aldrovandi per la sua villa di campagna', in *Documentary Culture: Florence and Rome from Grand-Duke Ferdinando I to Pope Alexander VII*, ed. Elizabeth Cropper, Giovanni Perini and Francesco Solinas (Bologna, 1992), pp. 317–48; Paula Findlen, *Possessing Nature: Museums, Collecting, and Scientific Culture in Early Modern Italy* (Berkeley and Los Angeles, CA, 1994), pp. 305–9; Lucia Corrain, 'Due scienziati bolognesi tra narrazione e autorappresentazione: Ulisse Aldrovandi e Anna Morandi Manzolini', *Schede umanistiche*, n.s., XXXIV/1 (2020), pp. 89–121, and 'Il manoscritto 99 di Ulisse Aldrovandi. Il programma iconografico della residenza di campagna', *Aldrovandiana*, 1/1 (2022), pp. 35–79.

57 Acciarino, *Lettere sulle grottesche*, pp. 91–8.

58 Clovis Whitfield, 'A Programme for *Erminia and the Shepherds* by G. B. Agucchi', *Storia dell'arte*, XIX (1973), pp. 217–29, and Eugenio Battisti, *L'antirinascimento*, 2nd edn (Turin, 2005), pp. 903–23.

59 Olmi, *L'inventario del mondo*, pp. 70–71.

60 Findlen, *Possessing Nature*, p. 309.

61 Roberto Zapperi, *Il selvaggio gentiluomo: l'incredibile storia di Pedro Gonzalez e dei suoi figli* (Rome, 2005), p. 82.

62 Giovanni Fantuzzi, *Memorie della vita di Ulisse Aldrovandi* (Bologna, 1774), p. 143; Patrizia Cavazzini, *Porta Virtutis: il processo a Federico Zuccari* (Rome, 2020), p. 79.

63 Acciarino, *Lettere sulle grottesche*, p. 98.

64 Olmi, *L'inventario del mondo*, p. 227.

65 Tosi, *Ulisse Aldrovandi e la Toscana*, p. 407.

7 *Ornithologia* and After: The Collection
  and the Posthumous Publications

1 The wren appears under this name, with a reference to Aldrovandi, in a catalogue of the animals kept in the Ashmolean Museum in 1695. Arthur MacGregor and Moira Hook, *Ashmolean Museum*

Oxford: Manuscript Catalogues of the Early Museum Collections (Part 11);
The Vice-Chancellor's Consolidated Catalogue 1695 (Oxford, 2006),
p. 93.

2   Laurent Pinon, 'Entre compilation et observation: l'écriture de
    l'Ornithologie d'Ulisse Aldrovandi', Genesis (Manuscrits-Recherche-
    Invention), XX (2003), pp. 53–70.

3   Aldrovandi to Clusius, 3 April 1590, Leiden University Library,
    VUL 101.

4   Aldrovandi to Clusius, 20 March 1591, ibid.

5   Giuseppe Olmi, L'inventario del mondo: catalogazione della natura e luoghi del
    sapere nella prima età moderna (Bologna, 1992), p. 33.

6   Antonio Battistella, Il S. Officio e la riforma religiosa in Bologna (Bologna,
    1905), p. 120 n. 2.

7   Francesco Solinas, L'Uccelliera: un libro di arte e di scienza nella Roma dei
    primi Lincei (Florence, 2000), p. 9.

8   Olmi, L'inventario del mondo, p. 27.

9   Francesco Solinas, 'Percorsi puteani: Note naturalistiche ed inediti
    appunti antiquari', in Cassiano dal Pozzo: atti del seminario internazionale
    di studi, ed. Francesco Solinas (Rome, 1989), pp. 95–129, here p. 98
    n. 17.

10 Peter Mason, Before Disenchantment: Images of Exotic Animals and Plants in
    the Early Modern World (London, 2009), p. 148.

11 Caroline Duroselle-Melish and David A. Lines, 'The Library of
    Ulisse Aldrovandi (†1605): Acquiring and Organizing Books in
    Sixteenth-Century Bologna', The Library, 7th series, XVI/2 (2015),
    pp. 133–61.

12 The woodblocks of images prepared for the publications are
    now divided between the two institutions: 1,822 in Museo
    di Palazzo Poggi, 1,950 in the University Library. See Fulvio
    Simoni, 'La natura incisa nel legno: la collezione delle matrici
    xilografiche di Ulisse Aldrovandi conservata all'Università di
    Bologna', Memofonte, XVII (2016), pp. 129–43; Fulvio Simoni,
    'Dal disegno al libro a stampa: la rappresentazione del mondo
    naturale nelle matrici xilografiche di Ulisse Aldrovandi', in
    Ulisse Aldrovandi: libri e immagini di storia naturale nella prima età moderna,
    ed. Giuseppe Olmi and Fulvio Simoni (Bologna, 2018),
    pp. 59–70.

13 Catalogo de' capi d'opera di pittura, scultura, antichità, libri, storia naturale
    ed altre curiosità trasportati dall'Italia in Francia (Venice, 1799),
    pp. xxx–xxxi.

14 Olmi, *L'inventario del mondo*, p. 45 n. 81.
15 Andrea Ubriszy Savoia, 'Le piante americane nell'Erbario di Ulisse
    Aldrovandi', *Webbia: Journal of Plant Taxonomy and Geography*, XLVIII
    (1993), pp. 579–98.
16 *Tavole*, BUB, 004/3-58 is dated 1612, 004/3-67 is dated 1614.
17 Laurent Pinon, 'Portrait emblématique du parfait mécène:
    Comment Ulisse Aldrovandi remercie le cardinal Montalto',
    in *Conflicting Duties: Science, Medicine and Religion in Rome, 1550–1750*,
    ed. Maria Pia Donato and Jill Kraye (Turin, 2009), pp. 59–88.
18 Giuseppe Olmi and Lucia Tongiorgi Tomasi, 'Dopo Ulisse
    Aldrovandi: migrazioni di immagini', in *Ulisse Aldrovandi: libri e
    immagini di storia naturale nella prima età moderna*, ed. Giuseppe Olmi and
    Fulvio Simoni (Bologna, 2018), pp. 9–21; José Ramón Marcaida,
    'Echoes of Aldrovandi: Notes on an Illustrated Album from the
    Natural History Museum in London', ibid., pp. 23–7.
19 Fabien Montcher, personal communication, 21 September 2021; and
    his 'Intellectuals for Hire: Iberian Men of Letters and Papal Politics
    in Bologna during the Thirty Years' War', in *Dimensioni e problemi della
    ricerca storica 11*, ed. Elena Valeri and Paola Volpini (2019), pp. 179–210.
20 Ian Rolfe and Alessandro Ceregato, '"A fossilized nut?": A Drawing
    from Aldrovandi in the Paper Museum of Cassiano dal Pozzo',
    Archives of Natural History, XXXVI/1 (2009), pp. 160–67.
21 Elizabeth McGrath, *Corpus Rubenianum XIII: Rubens Subjects from History*
    (London, 1997), vol. I, pp. 60–61.
22 Paula Findlen, *Possessing Nature: Museums, Collecting, and Scientific Culture in
    Early Modern Italy* (Berkeley and Los Angeles, CA, 1994), p. 27.
23 Joachium Camerarius, *Symbolorum et Emblematum ex volatilibus et insectis
    desumtorum [sic] centuria tertia collecta* (Nuremberg, 1596), emblem LIV.
24 Giuseppe Olmi, 'Per la storia dei rapporti scientifici fra Italia e
    Germania: le lettere di Francesco Calzolari a Joachim Camerarius
    II', in *Dai cantieri della storia: liber amicorum per Paolo Prodi*, ed. Gian Paolo
    Brizzi and Giuseppe Olmi (Bologna, 2007), pp. 343–61.
25 Giuseppe Gabriele, *Contributi alla storia della Accademia dei Lincei*
    (Rome, 1989), pp. 1084–7.
26 Mason, *Before Disenchantment*, pp. 149–54.
27 Solinas, *L'Uccelliera*; Paula Findlen, 'Cassiano dal Pozzo: A Roman
    Virtuoso in Search of Nature', in *Birds, Other Animals and Natural
    Curiosities: The Paper Museum of Cassiano dal Pozzo; A Catalogue Raisonné,
    Series B – Natural History, Parts 4 and 5*, vol. I, ed. Henrietta McBurney
    et al. (London, 2017), pp. 18–42.

28 Giovanni Pietro Olina, *L'Uccelliera ovvero discorso della natura e proprietà di diversi uccelli* [Rome, 1622] (Florence, 2000), p. 24. Not all copies of the 1622 edition include this plate.

29 *The Paper Museum of Cassiano dal Pozzo*, exh. cat., British Museum, London (1993), pp. 166–7; Jean-François Lhote and Danielle Joyal, eds, *Peiresc: Lettres à Cassiano dal Pozzo, 1626–1637* (Clermont-Ferrand, 1989), pp. 44, 51 and 53–6.

30 Giuseppe Gabriele, *Il carteggio linceo* (Rome, 1996), pp. 1191 and 1176; Irene Baldriga, *L'occhio della lince: i primi Lincei tra arte, scienza e collezionismo, 1603–1630* (Rome, 2002), pp. 236–7.

31 Cassiano to Peiresc, 26 September 1634, cited by Paula Findlen, 'Cassiano's Animals: Mammals, Fishes and Crustaceans in the Paper Museum', in *Birds, Other Animals and Natural Curiosities*, vol. II, pp. 480–96, here p. 496 n. 67.

32 Enrica Stendardo, *Ferrante Imperato: collezionismo e studio della natura a Napoli tra Cinque e Seicento* (Naples, 2001), pp. 75 and 138; Letizia Gaeta and Stefano De Mieri, *Intagliatori incisori scultori sodalizi e società nella Napoli dei viceré* (Galatina, 2015), p. 140.

33 Baldriga, *L'occhio della lince*, pp. 235–7.

34 Laurent Pinon, 'Clématite bleue contre poissons séchées: sept lettres inédites d'Ippolito Salviani à Ulisse Aldrovandi', *Mélanges de l'École française de Rome: Italie et la Méditerrannée*, CXIV/2 (2002), pp. 477–92.

35 See also Athanasius Kircher, *Mundus subterraneus* (Amsterdam, 1664), vol. VIII, pp. 38–9.

36 For the distinction see José Ramón Marcaida López, *Arte y ciencias en el barroco español* (Madrid, 2014), p. 33.

37 A complete modern facsimile edition with translation and accompanying essays has been published by Siloé ediciones, Burgos.

38 Michel Hochmann, ed., *Villa Medici: il sogno di un cardinale; collezioni e artisti di Ferdinando de' Medici*, exh. cat., Accademia di Francia a Roma, Rome (1999), cat. no. 30; Paolo Liverani and Giandomenico Spinola, *Vaticano 4: La Sala degli Animali nel Museo Pio-Clementino* (Milan, 2003), pp. 28 and 88–90. The original head is now in the Galleria degli Uffizi, Florence.

39 Sandra Tugnoli Pattaro, *Metodo e sistema delle scienze nel pensiero di Ulisse Aldrovandi* (Bologna, 1981), p. 141.

40 Olmi, *L'inventario del mondo*, p. 103.

41 Ibid., p. 33.

42 Thomas Browne, 'Tract I: Observations upon Several Plants Mention'd in Scripture' and 'Tract XIII: Musæum Clausum, or

Bibliotheca Abscondita', in *Certain Tracts* (London, 1684), pp. 48–9 and 193–215.

43 MacGregor and Hook, *Manuscript Catalogues of the Early Museum Collections*, pp. 93–106.

44 Margarita Vázquez Manassero, personal communication, April 2021.

45 Lisbet Koerner, *Linnaeus: Nature and Nation* (Cambridge, MA, and London, 1999), p. 34.

46 BM Prints and Drawings, painting 1; Kim Sloan, 'Sloane's "pictures and drawings in frames" and "books of miniatures & painting, designs, &c."', in *From Books to Bezoars: Sir Hans Sloane and His Collections*, ed. Alison Walker, Arthur MacGregor and Michael Hunter (London, 2012), pp. 168–89, here p. 178. On Sloane and his collection, also see Arthur MacGregor, ed., *Sir Hans Sloane: Collector, Scientist, Antiquary* (London, 1994).

47 Veronica Carpita and Elena Vaiani, eds, *La correspondance de Nicolas-Claude Fabri de Peiresc avec Lelio Pasqualini, 1601–1611, et son neveu Pompeo, 1613–1622* (Paris, 2012), p. 7, n. 38.

48 Frédérique Lemerle, 'Nicolas-Claude Fabri de Peiresc et les ruines romaines', in *Peiresc et l'Italie*, ed. Marc Fumaroli (Paris, 2009), pp. 205–18.

49 Isabelle de Conihout, 'Du nouveau sur la bibliothèque de Peiresc', ibid., pp. 243–63, here p. 246; Lorenzo Baldacchini, 'La diffusione e la fortuna dei libri di Ulisse Aldrovandi in area francofona', in *Ulisse Aldrovandi: libri e immagini di storia naturale nella prima età moderna*, ed. Giuseppe Olmi and Fulvio Simoni (Bologna, 2018), pp. 119–23.

50 Amanda Claridge and Ian Jenkins, 'Cassiano and the Tradition of Drawing from the Antique', in *The Paper Museum of Cassiano dal Pozzo*, pp. 13–26.

51 Florike Egmond, 'Looking Beyond the Margins of Print: Depicting Water Creatures in Europe, *c.* 1500–1620', in *Towards a Cultural History of Early Modern Ichthyology, 1500–1800*, ed. Paul J. Smith and Florike Egmond (Leiden, forthcoming).

52 Miguel de Cervantes, *Segunda parte del ingenioso cavallero Don Quixote de La Mancha* (Madrid, 1615), Chapter 68.

53 Jean Céard, *La Nature et les prodiges* (Geneva, 1996), p. 455.

54 Georges-Louis Leclerc, comte de Buffon, *Histoire naturelle, générale et particulière, avec la description du cabinet du Roi* (Paris, 1749–67), vol. 1, p. 26, cited in Baldacchini, 'La diffusione et la fortuna', p. 119.

55 William B. Ashworth, 'Emblematic Natural History of the
    Renaissance', in *Cultures of Natural History*, ed. Nicholas Jardine, Anne
    Secord and Emma Spary (Cambridge, 1996), pp. 17–37, here pp. 33–4.

56 Eugenio Battisti, *L'antirinascimento*, 2nd edn (Turin, 2005), p. 669.

57 Michel Foucault, *Les mots et les choses* (Paris, 1966), pp. 40 and 106.

58 Irina Podgorny, *Florentino Ameghino y hermanos: empresa argentina de
    paleontología ilimitada* (Buenos Aires, 2021), p. 139.

59 Giuseppe Olmi, 'Science-Honour-Metaphor: Italian Cabinets of
    the Sixteenth and Seventeenth Centuries', in *The Origins of Museums*,
    ed. Oliver Impey and Arthur MacGregor (Oxford, 1985), pp. 5–16;
    Laura Laurencich-Minelli, 'Museography and Ethnographical
    Collections in Bologna during the Sixteenth and Seventeenth
    Centuries', ibid., pp. 17–23.

SELECT BIBLIOGRAPHY

Alessandrini, Alessandro, and Alessandro Ceregato, eds,
    Natura picta: Ulisse Aldrovandi, (Bologna, 2007) (with *c.* 500
    colour plates)
Céard, Jean, *La Nature et les prodiges: l'insolite au XVIe siècle* (Geneva, 1996)
Cecchi, Alessandro, Lucilia Conigliello and Marzia Faietti, eds, *Jacopo
    Ligozzi 'pittore universalissimo'*, exh. cat., Palazzo Pitti, Florence
    (Livorno, 2014)
Egmond, Florike, *The World of Carolus Clusius: Natural History in the Making,
    1550–1610* (London, 2010)
——, Lucia Tongiorgi Tomasi, Giuseppe Olmi and Peter Mason,
    eds *Das Naturalienkabinett des Ulisse Aldrovandi. 2500 Aquarelltafeln
    aus dem 16. Jahrhundert* (Darmstadt, 2023)
Findlen, Paula, *Possessing Nature: Museums, Collecting, and Scientific Culture
    in Early Modern Italy* (Berkeley and Los Angeles, CA, 1994)
Friedman, John B., *The Monstrous Races in Medieval Art and Thought*
    (Cambridge and London, 1981)
Horodowich, Elizabeth, and Lia Markey, eds, *The New World in Early
    Modern Italy, 1492–1750* (Cambridge, 2017)
Impey, Oliver, and Arthur MacGregor, *The Origins of Museums* (Oxford,
    1985)
Laurencich-Minelli, Laura, 'From the New World to Bologna, 1533:
    A Gift to Pope Clement VII and Bolognese Collections of the
    Sixteenth and Seventeenth Centuries', *Journal of the History of
    Collections*, XXIV/2 (2012), pp. 145–58
——, ed., *Bologna e il mondo nuovo*, exh. cat., Museo Civico Medievale,
    Bologna (1992)
Mason, Peter, and José Pardo-Tomás, 'Bringing It Back from Mexico:
    Eleven Paintings of Trees in *I cinque libri delle piante* of Pier'Antonio

Michiel, 1510–1576', *Journal of the History of Collections*, XXXII/2 (2020), pp. 225–37

Olmi, Giuseppe, *L'inventario del mondo: catalogazione della natura e luoghi del sapere nella prima età moderna* (Bologna, 1992)

—, '"Molti amici in varij luoghi": studio della natura e rapporti epistolari nel secolo XVI', *Nuncius*, VI (1991), pp. 3–11

—, 'Science and the Court: Some Comments on "Patronage" in Italy', in *Science and Power: The Historical Foundations of Research Policies in Europe*, ed. Luca Guzzetti (Florence, 1994), pp. 25–45

—, and Fulvio Simoni, eds, *Ulisse Aldrovandi: libri e immagini di storia naturale nella prima età moderna* (Bologna, 2018)

Digital Resources

The following resources can be found at http://aldrovandi.dfc.unibo.it/pinakesweb/main.asp:

Catalogue of the manuscripts of Ulisse Aldrovandi kept in the University Library of Bologna
Aldrovandi's coloured drawings (*Tavole*)
Correspondence (selected items in transcription)
Aldrovandi's *Discorso naturale*
Images of Ulisse Aldrovandi
Edition of the biography by Giovanni Fantuzzi (1774)

All of the woodblocks cut for printing the publications of Ulisse Aldrovandi, kept in Palazzo Poggi, Bologna, can be found at http://ibc.regione.emilia-romagna.it.

ACKNOWLEDGEMENTS

First and foremost, my most heartfelt thanks to Giuseppe Olmi and Lucia Tongiorgi Tomasi, whose spot-on, lightning replies to my queries left me feeling like Dante's Belacqua. Florike Egmond and Arthur MacGregor read the whole text and suggested a number of improvements. Thanks are also due for their assistance in various ways to Kim Sloan, Davide Domenici, Fulvio Simoni and the two readers for Reaktion Books. Finally, I would particularly like to thank Giacomo Nerozzi and the photographic department of the Biblioteca Universitaria di Bologna for the kind permission to reproduce 26 coloured drawings from the Aldrovandi collection held in that institution.

PHOTO ACKNOWLEDGEMENTS

The author and publishers wish to express their thanks to the below sources of illustrative material and/or permission to reproduce it. Some locations of artworks are also given below, in the interest of brevity:

Accademia Carrara, Bergamo: 1; from Ulisse Aldrovandi, *De piscibus libri V et De cetis lib. unus* (Bologna, 1638), photos Wellcome Collection, London: 36, 37; from Ulisse Aldrovandi, *De quadrupedibus digitatis viviparis libri tres* (Bologna, 1645), photo Wellcome Collection, London: 60; from Ulisse Aldrovandi, *Monstrorum historia cum Paralipomena accuratissima historiae omnium animalium* (Bologna, 1642), photos Wellcome Collection, London: 23, 24, 32, 39, 42, 44, 45, 48, 50, 57; from Ulisse Aldrovandi, *Musaeum metallicum in libros IIII distributum* (Bologna, 1648), photos Getty Research Institute, Los Angeles: 8, 25, 26, 27, 28, 29, 51, 52, 55, 56; from Ulisse Aldrovandi, *Ornithologiae hoc est de avibus historiae libri XII* (Bologna, 1599), photos Library of Congress, Washington, DC: 16, 18, 19, 21, 41; from Ulisse Aldrovandi, *Ornithologiae tomus alter* (Bologna, 1600), photo Library of Congress, Washington, DC: 63; from Ulisse Aldrovandi, *Quadrupedum omnium bisulcorum historia* (Bologna, 1621), photos Wellcome Collection, London: 67, 68; from Ulisse Aldrovandi, *Serpentum et draconum historiae libri duo*, vol. I (Bologna, 1640), photo Wellcome Collection, London: 49; © Alma Mater Studiorum Università di Bologna – Biblioteca Universitaria di Bologna (MS 124): 5 (*Tavole di animali*, vol. VII, c. 131), 9 (*Tavole di animali*, vol. IV, c. 43), 10 (*Tavole di animali*, vol. IV, c. 60), 11 (*Tavole di animali*, vol. III, c. 140), 14 (*Tavole di animali*, vol. IV, c. 132), 15 (*Tavole di animali*, vol. I, c. 159), 17 (*Tavole di piante*, vol. X, c. 7), 20 (*Tavole di animali*, vol. I, c. 74), 22 (*Tavole di animali*, vol. I, c. 75), 30 (*Tavole di piante*, vol. I, c. 70), 31 (*Tavole di piante*, vol. III, c. 196), 33 (*Tavole di animali*, vol. V, c. 86), 34 (*Tavole di animali*, vol. IV, c. 121), 35 (*Tavole di animali*, vol. IV, c. 122), 40 (*Tavole di animali*, vol. VI, c. 92), 43 (*Tavole di animali*, vol. I, c. 132), 46 (*Tavole di animali*, vol. IV, c. 130), 47 (*Tavole di animali*, vol. IV, c. 117/A), 53 (*Tavole di animali*, vol. V, c. 139), 54 (*Tavole di animali*, vol. VII, c. 63), 58 (*Tavole di animali*, vol. VI, c. 87), 59 (*Tavole di animali*, vol. V, c. 33), 61 (*Tavole di piante*, vol. X, c. 3), 62 (*Tavole di animali*, vol. II, c. 155), 65 (*Tavole di piante e animali*, vol. IV, c. 72); from Pierre Belon, *Les observations de plusieurs singularitez et choses memorables trouvées en Grèce, Asie, Judée,* Égypte, *Arabie et autres pays estranges* (Paris, 1553), photo Getty Research Institute, Los Angeles: 7; Bibliothèque municipale de Nantes: 38 (MS fr. 8, fol. 163v); from Benedetto Ceruti, *Musaeum Franc. Calceolarii iun. Veronensis a Benedicto Ceruto medico incaeptum* (Verona, 1622), photo Smithsonian Libraries, Washington, DC: 2; © Château royal de Blois (photo François Lauginie): 64; from Ferrante Imperato, *Dell'historia naturale* (Naples, 1599), photo Wellcome Collection, London: 12; photos Peter Mason: 3, 6; The Metropolitan Museum of Art, New York: 4; Museo Nazionale del Bargello, Florence (photo © Ben Rimmer): 13; from Giovanni Pietro Olina, *Uccelliera overo discorso della natura e proprieta di diversi uccelli . . .* (Rome, 1622), photo Getty Research Institute: 66.

INDEX

Illustration numbers are indicated by *italics*.